HAPPINESS
$10 ON A DAY

HAPPINESS $10 ON A DAY

A RECESSION-PROOF GUIDE

Heather Wagner

Illustrations by Mike Perry

HARPER

NEW YORK • LONDON • TORONTO • SYDNEY

HarperCollins books may be purchased for educational, business, or sales promotional use. For information, please write: Special Markets Department, HarperCollins Publishers, 10 East 53rd Street, New York, NY 10022.

FIRST EDITION

Designed by Ashley Halsey

Library of Congress Cataloging-in-Publication Data

Wagner, Heather.
    Happiness on $10 a day : a recession-proof guide / Heather Wagner ;
illustrations by Mike Perry.—1st ed.
    p. cm.
    ISBN 978-0-06-177880-3
    1. Consumer education. 2. Thriftiness. I. Title. II. Title: Happiness on
ten dollars a day.
TX335.W235 2009
640.73—dc22   2009003832

09 10 11 12 13 OV/RRD   10 9 8 7 6 5 4 3 2 1

Acknowledgments

I would like to thank Stephanie Meyers, Maya Rock, Mike Perry, friends and family who inspired this material, and Andrew, who, along with roasted chicken, red wine, and goose-down pillows, is a steadfast happiness provider.

CONTENTS

About the Author and Illustrator

INTRODUCTION

Happiness. We're all desperate to get there, but it's not a journey with crisply illuminated road signs. As with Mapquest, the more closely you stick to the written directions, the farther you end up from where you want to go.

Expectations are the roadblocks to happiness, the orange construction barrels that hinder your journey. Think of the hotly anticipated vacation that falls apart: the bedbugs, the sunburn, the arguing over pay-per-view. You look back at those early, optimistic drinks at the airport and think, "That was the best part of the trip!" And you are right.

So consider this book a tour guide for the detours and often-overlooked backroads of life's most desirable and yet most elusive destination. It doesn't have to be a costly journey; you'll see that life can be fully explored and enjoyed without extravagance or, in some cases, without even leaving your bed. With just ten dollars a day (sometimes a little more, sometimes a little less), you can find happiness in places both surprising and obvious. Consider this your license to indulge, a commandment to stop and smell the rosé, an instructional guide for seizing the moments—major and minor—that bring you an unambiguous rush of well-being, without breaking the bank.

And since very few people find happiness in an overlong introduction, with that said, let's get on with the book. Happy travels!

—The Author

SHORTCUTS TO HAPPINESS

Everybody loves a shortcut, so here is a handy happiness icon system for quick happiness hunting:

 A Time for Personal Reflection and Musing

 Artistic Expression May Occur

 Boozy Fun

Get Crafty!

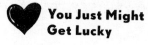 You Just Might Get Lucky

Hilarity Is Assured

This Activity Rocks So Hard!

Acting Skills Necessary

Religious Enlightenment? Possibly.

Cute Animals

Soothing Activity

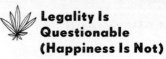

AFFORDABILITY RATING

*Additionally, each entry will feature an affordability rating (**FREE!, $, $$, $$$,** and **$$$$**) designating the budget-friendly (or -unfriendly) nature of each happiness-providing activity.*

1

flying solo

Find happiness spending quality time with your favorite person—you

"Most folks are about as happy as they make up their minds to be."

—ABRAHAM LINCOLN

Searching for a charming, insightful, and knowing companion that really gets you? Look in the mirror. Sometimes appreciating your own company is the quickest and easiest path to happiness.

BENCHING (FREE!)

   A select few find happiness while free-climbing, kayaking, or running a triathlon. But the sane majority of us can get just as much of a rush from, say, finding the right bench. "Benching," a hot new hybrid sport combining sitting and staring, can be your ticket to hours of contentment.

Bench selection is a crucial factor to consider. Optimally, your bench will be facing an area with some activity (attractive strangers, lapping waves, warbling birds) but not too much (screaming children, crackheads, cement mixers). It will have an equal mixture of sun and shade and will not be emblazoned with a Cialis advertisement. It should have a shallow pitch, sturdy wooden-construction, and a slight curvature. There is a wide world of benching accessories to choose from, the most important of which is the thermos. There's just something about a thermos and bench that go together. Stick with the old-school kind (Thermos brand for a classic look, Stanley for that lunching-construction-worker vibe) and fill it with the beverage of your choice: coffee, chicken soup, Dark 'n Stormys. Another key accessory is reading material. Nothing beats a newspaper, but a paperback novel is also a nice touch—the bendier the book's spine, the better. Finish off with a pocketful of breadcrumbs and you have yourself a day of free entertainment.

LOOK MYSTERIOUS AT A CAFÉ ($–$$)

Solo dining can be tough. Swanky restaurants view you as a social outcast or nefarious food blogger. Diners and coffee shops are full of, respectively, depressing old people and irritating laptop hipsters. Eating in front of the TV with your pants off is the type of thing that wears you down over time. In the middle of this spectrum lies the lively, enduring café—the gift of the Europeans, who know how to live!

The keys to true café solo happiness are location and time

of day. Choose an under-the-radar location. How to tell if it's under-the-radar? Is there a celebrity chef, children's Playplace, or all-you-can-drink mojito special? Keep moving. Look for old tiles, a top-quality espresso machine, and faded umbrellas. If your town lacks such an establishment, a low-key lunch spot or particularly plush Starbucks will do. Midafternoon is the best time to frequent a café. The lighting is right, ordering wine isn't frowned upon, and there are no awkward post-one-night-stand brunches or actual dates in progress.

To round out your experience, and cultivate the maximum allure and mystery, be sure to:

- Bring a book, journal, or weighty, serious publication, taking care that these accessories encourage musing (e.g., *On the Road*, not *The Best of Sudoku*; *The Paris Review*, not *USA Today*; a Moleskine notebook, not a stack of Excel spreadsheets).
- Wear sunglasses, even indoors.
- Order an espresso or cappuccino, *never* a latte, smoothie, or mocha-frappé.
- Frown slightly.
- Rest your chin on your fist occasionally.
- Smoke, if applicable. Sigh, if not.

Sit back, and let *le mystère* unfold!

SAY GOODBYE TO GUILT (FREE!)

 Guilt is an unfortunate byproduct of questionable activity—the spiritual indigestion after one of life's proverbial chili dogs. But does guilt serve any purpose other than making us feel shifty and low? Does torturing yourself and wondering "Why, *why*?" make you a better person? Probably not. Here are a few ways to say au revoir to this self-destructive emotion and bonjour to a happier, guilt-free you.

Put It in Perspective

Unless you did something really, really bad, use the trusty "Grander Scheme of Things" clause to abate your guilt. Think about how many people live on the planet (currently 6,665,767,978) and how little your actions have affected any of them. There's a young woman in Quito on her way to the fish market who does not care that you called your boss's wife "unfortunate looking" within earshot, just as there is a hundred-year-old yogi in Phuket who is staring at a stucco wall, utterly unaware that you forgot your mother's birthday (again) or spent the rest of your grant money on drugs. In recognizing the minimal impact of your behavior in the Grander Scheme of Things, you can relax and truly believe that whatever you did just wasn't that big of a deal.

Another angle on this is the time-heals-all-wounds tactic, "In ten years, nobody will care about this." Try to think of something that happened ten years ago. It's pretty hard to recall specifics, right? Even if someone did something unspeakably rude, are you still *actively* angry at them? Unlikely. A final handy mental exercise is the versatile, "Everyone else was too drunk to notice."

Visualize and Conquer

Give your guilt an avatar—a visual representation that is annoying enough to irk and trouble you but not flat-out evil or scary:

Buzzing Mosquito

Ill-Fitting Pair of Slacks

Caffeine-Free Diet Soda

City Tow Truck

Sleet/Wintry Mix

Howie Mandel

AOL

Lukewarm Sushi

Next, transfer all of your guilty feelings to this pesky nuisance. Then—swat, incinerate, crush, dispose of, delete, or run it through the bad-slacks paper shredder. Problem solved!

AMATEUR MIXOLOGY ($–$$)

The artisanal cocktail trend is certainly fun—the exotic reductions and elixirlike combinations of odd ingredients (like ginger, egg white, and bitters) add insiders-only elitism to the practice of getting sloshed. But specialty cocktails are just so expensive—$12–$16 at most urban prohibition-chic dens. Fear not, decadent boozehounds—you can beat the system.

Knowing how to make and serve specialty cocktails on a moment's notice takes practice, but in time you'll be serving up Ramos fizzes with the best of them. Here are a few happiness-inducing cocktails that will have your roommates, neighbors, and significant others clamoring for access to the hip, underground lounge that is your living room:

✗ Classic Caipirinha

2 Tahitian limes
caster sugar
crushed ice

1 ½ ounces good-quality
cachaça

If your days on the international club circuit are waning and you seek the quiet consolation of a "me cocktail" after a tough week, the classic caipirinha creates the perfect balance of sweetness and acidity, as well as an unmistakable air of South American joie de vivre.

To Prepare: Muddle limes (try Tahitian limes, which are slightly sweeter than their Mexican counterparts) with a wooden muddler, then add caster sugar, ice, and cachaça. Mix and serve in a sugar-rimmed lowball glass with DJ Gilles Peterson or Caetano Veloso.

Recession Version: Substitute good-quality cachaça with bottom-shelf rum, mix with 7-Up over ice, and serve with Telemundo.

✗ Elderflower Martini

St Germain elderflower liqueur
½ fresh-pressed lime
ice

½ ounces white wine
mint sprig

The elderflower martini is, frankly, a girl drink. If the white wine and elderflower cordial aren't enough, the mint sprig seals it. But don't let stale old Victorian gender mores get you down. Remember that it's all in how you carry yourself. If you're a sharply dressed man with an elderflower martini in one hand, and an Oprah's Book Club selection in the other, ladies might view you as someone sensitive who will listen and really understand (read: gay). However, pair this bracing, tart, and sweet cocktail with a cigar or handgun and hello, James Bond!

To Prepare: Shake St Germain and lime juice over ice in a chilled ice shaker. Serve in a martini glass with prosecco or white wine floater. Garnish with a mint sprig or lemon twist and serve with Serge Gainsbourg.

Recession Version: Replace elderflower liqueur with Boone's Farm Apple Blossom or Melon Ball (very few people can correctly identify elderflower, anyway) and serve with your abandoned French language tapes.

✕ The Bloody-Everything-But-The-Kitchen-Sink Mary

lime wedges	tomato juice
celery salt	Tabasco sauce
black pepper	Worcestershire sauce
fresh basil leaves	cherry tomatoes
1 ounce decent-quality vodka	green olives

Perfect for the hungover, the salt-deficient, and the brave few who believe that the Bloody Mary is not just for brunch. It takes a confident sort to whip one up at 9 p.m., but what is life for if not shaking off the shackles of convention? Plus, a vigorously accessorized Bloody Mary is essentially a meal. Remember, there is much food value in booze but no booze value in food.

To Prepare: Rim a pint glass with lime juice, then dip the rim into a mixture of celery salt and black pepper. Muddle the fresh basil leaves, then add vodka, tomato juice, lime juice, Tabasco, and Worcestershire. Garnish with cherry tomatoes and green olives and serve with a Wes Anderson movie.

Recession Version: Swap out "decent-quality vodka" with "barely passable vodka" (the spiciness masks the flavor, anyhow) and serve with a nice view of the trees outside your window.

✖ Suddenly Sangria

(Recipe courtesy of Stacy Slinkard)

1 bottle cheapo red wine (Cabernet, Rioja, Shiraz, boxed)
1 lemon cut into wedges
1 orange cut into wedges
1 lime cut into wedges

2 tablespoons sugar
splash of orange juice
2 ounces halfway decent gin
1 cup sliced raspberries
4 cups ginger ale

Sangria is great because it uses everyday ingredients and can be made and served in bulk—the Costco of cocktails. Like the Bloody Mary, it also has some nutritional value, and is far less tragic than nursing your bottle of cheap Australian Shiraz over *Grey's Anatomy* reruns. Note: spicy/salty almonds make a brilliant counterpart to the sweetness.

To Prepare: Pour wine into a large pitcher, squeeze in fruit, then add the spent fruit wedges, OJ, and gin. Chill for at least an hour. Add ginger ale, ice, and berries just before serving. Serve with Shakira or Buena Vista Social Club. (No recession version necessary!)

✖ Create Your Own Specialty Cocktail

whatever's around the liquor cabinet and/or spice rack

It's high time you had a specialty cocktail created by you and named in your honor.

Search through your collection of booze and spices and do a little at-home experimenting. One finger of Captain Morgan + cinnamon stick + steamed milk = Wendy's Winter WonderDrink. Splash of triple sec + shot of Cuervo + cayenne pepper + ice = Mike's Madman Margarita. Write down your recipe for posterity and try peering at it through a pince-nez before serving to get in the mixologist mood.

WRITE A STERNLY WORDED LETTER (FREE!-$)

In these days of clipped electronic communication, the cathartic release of a sternly worded letter is all but lost. Sure, you may be able to get your point across via sharp-thumbed Blackberry, thorny Facebook wall post, or bitchy email, but all of these pale in comparison to an eloquently expressed, carefully typed, and elegantly signed missive. Think of someone or something that deserves your vitriol. The cable company. Your ex. Your upstairs neighbor who plays the Moody Blues all weekend long. Squeeze your rage into short, pithy paragraphs, state your case with logic and grace, and don't sleep on it—you need to get this baby stamped and in the mailbox before you lose your nerve. The upside of the Sternly Worded Letter, besides the fact that you have now "put it in writing," is that results, while slower to arrive, will usually be of a more impressive magnitude. The cable company may beg for your business back and offer you a reduced rate. Your ex may ball his or her fists in rage, realize what a mistaken, pathetic excuse for a life he or she has without you, and come crawling back. And your neighbor just might knock it off with the Moody Blues . . . or at least keep it to a reasonable volume. None of these things are guaranteed to result from your letter, but you can take a special sort of comfort knowing that your feelings are *out there* (while sparing yourself a record of them in your outbox to re-read obsessively for days to come.) Key words to use: *vehement, excruciating, diabolical, distressing, injustice, fallacy, breach.* Key phrases: "My patience is at its end," "Or else," and the always effective, "The next correspondence will be from my lawyers." Note that *lawyers*—plural—is always more effective.

Write a Love Letter (FREE!–$)

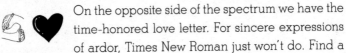 On the opposite side of the spectrum we have the time-honored love letter. For sincere expressions of ardor, Times New Roman just won't do. Find a nice piece of stationery, grab an ink pen, and write. You know, with your hand. Your cursive may be as wobbly and unsure as a third grader's, but there is no matching the personal touch of hand-dotted *i*'s, crossed *t*'s, and the creative takes on the English language brought about by the lack of spell-check.

Clichés are the basis for most love letters, so start there, but once you get in the groove, try to get original. Do not compare thee to a summer's day, but do consider a crisp Maine autumn morning or a steamy Bengalese sunset. If you count the ways in which you love them, make sure they're unique to your beloved's personality ("I love how your cute little nose wrinkles when you laugh, I love that you know how to roast a chicken") and include unexpected and sensitive takes on their physical beauty, as opposed to, "You have great tits." Extra points for authentic touches like tear stains, lipstick smudges, perfume, or cologne. Minus points for creepy or unsettling touches like locks of hair, blood-based ink, or a medieval candle-wax seal that bears your silhouette.

TURN BACK TIME . . . ON A DIME (FREE!–$$)

Getting old doesn't make anyone happy. Crow's-feet, stray grays, dull, weathered skin, bah! But you can feel young by acting young. The next time you hear yourself begin to say, "The problem with the Internet . . . ," "Remember when MTV played music?" or "Darn you kids, get off my lawn!" stop yourself and say something youthful and modern like "LOL" or "Isn't it time to retire the word 'Douchebag'?" Ask your young cousin who her favorite bands are and download a song or two. Instead of frequenting establishments that cater to the fake-ID crowd, start hanging around your city's cafeterias, all-you-can-eat early-bird buffets, and the saltiest dive bars—there's nothing like proximity to actual old people to make you feel twenty-two again.

COMPASSIONATE COMMUTING (FREE!–$)

If you happen to be on a train/bus/plane that has a delay of more than ten minutes, instead of suffering in silence, take this meditative time to break the invisible wall and comment on the inconvenience/incompetence of the airline/public transport system/bus driver. This forms an instant, and sometimes lasting, bond. Testing the waters for commuting rapport is low-risk, yet often yields large amounts of happiness. Your "subway friend" could become a stellar new recruit at your company; your Jet Blue seatmate might turn into your mate for life. Sometimes all you need is eye contact, an audible sigh, or an expression like, "Are they kidding?" or "Not again!" Even if your exchange lasts only for the duration of the delay, those precious minutes of mutual venting are not only cathartic, but they also enable you to feel a special solidarity—a feeling that we're really all brothers and sisters. It also gives you an unbeatable "how we met" story if things do get romantic.

FIND SOMEONE ELSE'S RELIGION (FREE!)

 Religion: you may be neutral about it or vaguely remember it from childhood. You may avoid it like the plague or have a safe and loving relationship with it, or you may be one of those people who gets "Jesus-y" and makes everyone a little uncomfortable. All of this is totally fine. In a world filled with so much dizzying possibility, how could we all be expected to believe in the exact same things? So ditch your uninformed assumptions and theological disagreements and get to know those chaps on the other side of the pew. You might learn something. You might be converted. You might feel enlightened. You might just be ready for lunch. But what's certain, is that one point or another, you will get a glimpse into someone else's idea of eternal happiness, which can be a form of happiness all its own.

What to Expect When You're Crashing a Service
Protestant (Presbyterian/Episcopalian/Lutheran/Methodist)
Unlike in the bleaker Puritan days, modern Protestant services often provide a less hellfire-focused form of Christianity. Sometimes there will be a youth choir or "rock" band to break up the monotony. You'll usually read from the New Testament, and sermons will be peppered with everyday anecdotes about soccer practice and technology. There is a part where you are asked to shake the hands of everyone around you and say,

"Peace be with you." It's a little uncomfortable, but you can handle it.

Catholic Catholic mass is more traditional and tends to stick to a more dogmatic program. Parts of it are sometimes in Latin, and there's lots of kneeling, silent prayer, and repeating after the priest. When in doubt say, "And also with you." The incense portion is a nice aromatic distraction, and you will usually be staring at a sculpture of a crucifixion in progress, so if you have a weak stomach, try to focus on the saints or pretty stained glass instead.

Jewish A great Jewish tradition is the viewing of curiosity as a noble trait, so if you're curious about Judaism, feel free to stop by your local synagogue. The focal point of the synagogue is the ark, a cabinet in the wall that holds the Torah scrolls, so get there early for a good view. During certain prayers, the doors and/or curtain of the ark may be opened or closed, and you're supposed to stand. A man should wear a yarmulke; in many cases yarmulkes are available at the entrance for those who don't come prepared. Also note: it helps if you can read backwards.

> **HAPPINESS HINT**
>
> Try to pick the most popular or innovative church in your city or town, or the church with the most architectural significance. This helps alleviate the sparsely-attended-service syndrome, in which you feel that the pastor is staring at you the whole time.

Mormon A Mormon chapel is different from a Mormon temple. Anyone can attend the former, but for the latter you must be a member of the church in "good standing" to attend. The chapel/free-for-all service begins with hymns and prayers, and then members receive a sacramental communion of bread and water, which you should pass on down the aisle if you are a non-Mormon. A few sermons, some prayers, and you're officially down with the LDS.

Quaker The great thing about Quakers is that everyone is a friend. (Literally—the congregants are referred to as "Friends.") Another thing you'll note about a Quaker church is that it isn't really a church. No booming organ music or Roman statues, instead the typical Quaker meeting space more closely resembles your local DMV. When the first person enters the room, the service has begun, until the room is full. This period is called "expectant waiting." Then, one by one, all Friends are encouraged to offer a "message," a spontaneous thought about faith. Try to avoid that talking-to-hear-yourself-talk sensation that plagues most indie film Q&A's.

Muslim Outside every mosque is a place where you can remove your shoes, sort of like an overly cautious hostess's cocktail party. That's where the similarity ends—the main hall of a mosque is a bare room largely devoid of furniture, and everyone sits on the floor. A niche in one of the walls, called a *mihrab*, shows the direction of Mecca, which you should face while praying. There are five prayers and five positions that you'll need to get in, so arrive limber. With so much peace, thankfulness, and solemnity, you will soon learn that Muslims are nothing to be afraid of, nor are they deserving of any tense stares at the airport.

Megachurch These Rick Warren-style monster truck rallies of faith take place in the suburbs and exurbs, and are host to many dudes in shorts and Hawaiian shirts and women who consider Sonic Burgers a food group. Worth experiencing firsthand, especially for the Sinbad-style comedic parables and reminders of what "real" America looks like, you betcha!

Buddhist Perhaps one of the trendier religions right now, Buddhism is based on the principle of impermanence, and the fundamental truth that life is always moving, flowing, and changing. Buddhists call this truth the "dharma." During a service, Buddhists join their hands together and bow their heads in deference to the dharma. There is a shrine to Buddha, which you'll be asked to bow toward; other ritual activities include offering incense, chanting texts from the sutras or singing hymns, and quiet meditation. You may now officially refer to yourself as "spiritual."

A random list of other religions to check out: Baha'i, Confucianism, Hinduism, Jainism, Shinto, Sikhism, Taoism, Celtic Druidism, Zoroastrianism, Mennonite, Greek Orthodox, Moravian, Wicca, Southern Baptist, Macumba, Voodoo, Unitarianism.

HAPPINESS HINT

No matter how informal the service, be sure to turn off your cell phone. Your Lil Wayne ringer is not typically considered a divine message.

HARASS A TELEMARKETER (FREE!)

When your home or cell phone rings and an unknown area code pops up, your first thought might be, "Do I have an ex that now lives in the 617 area code?" The second thought might be, "Uh oh, is that the credit card company/banker man/scary student loan collections person?" The third invariably is, "Goddamned telemarketer," and even if we know what's going to happen on the other end of the line, curiosity sometimes gets the best of us.

Here's what to do when you realize you've gotten stuck on the phone with an auto insurance specialist or Sunny Days Time Share representative: say that you would really like to speak with them and learn more about this special offer, but that the connection is bad. Ask them if they have a personal cell phone that you may call to fully take advantage of this once-in-a-lifetime opportunity. If you're lucky enough to get a dim-witted telemarketer who will actually share their digits, make a point to call them a few times a month, just to chat. Dinnertime is best. Think of topics that are personally relevant to you that have absolutely no bearing on this stranger's life. Your cat's funny habit of scratching the blinds, your love of QVC collectible jewelry, or the summer when you went to the river and thought you saw a water snake but it turned out to be a garden hose. This type of sweet revenge is sure to brighten your day, and, who knows, you might even make a friend.

GO ON A RIDE-ALONG, PONCH! (FREE!)

 The five-O, the popo, the pigs, the man, bacon . . . whatever term you might use to refer to officers of the law, it's likely not an overly complimentary one. But why not hop over that thin blue line and see what it's like to be law-enforcing, instead of law-evading, for an afternoon? Most precincts have a police ride-along program that allows citizens to accompany officers during their tour of duty in a police vehicle. The idea is to give civilians a better understanding of police operations. It will also give you superior cocktail party banter for months to come. All you need to do is to contact your local police precinct, fill out and fax a simple form, and be ready to hop into a patrol car for four to eight hours, where you'll basically be free to sit back and feel the power. Here are some dos and don'ts for your day of protecting and serving:

DO: Show up on time.

DON'T: Throw up any gang signs as a greeting or demand to change the radio station.

DO: Wear a seat belt.

DON'T: Chat up any victims, suspects, or witnesses during the day, even if you think your powers of persuasion just might "break" them.

DO: Dress nicely and conservatively, but also comfortably—as though you're about to go on a job interview for a gym receptionist position.

DON'T: Try to look coplike by growing a bushy Magnum P.I. mustache or sporting tinted aviators.

DO: Ask questions and appear engaged and alert.

DON'T: Complain about your recent speeding ticket or recite a lot of *Hawaii Five-O, CHiPs, Miami Vice,* or *Starsky and Hutch* dialogue.

DO: Offer to buy the officers lunch, doughnuts, or coffee.

DON'T: Offer to buy the officers a drink.

DO: Ask the officer to share stories of his years on the force.

DON'T: Ask if he or she has ever strip-searched someone.

DO: Inquire what sort of law enforcement weaponry he or she uses.

DON'T: Ask for a demonstration.

GET BACK TO NATURE, THE LAZY WAY (FREE!)

Getting in touch with nature is something we'd all like to do more of. It's free, it's fun, and it's a good way to take notice of this planet we live on. But sometimes "nature" as a concept can be overwhelming, especially for those stuck in strip mall suburbs or dense urban environs. Instead of getting hung up on grand plans of solo treks through the Andes, start small. Go for easy, accessible "nature firsts," and pledge to get outside to see the following:

The First Robin of Spring
The First Dandelion of Summer
The First Turning Leaf of Autumn
The First Snowflake of Winter

With these quarterly expeditions outside, you'll get in touch with nature and your neighborhood, feel connected to something greater, and get a happiness-producing but low-maintenance sense of peace and well-being. No compass or bulky shoes required.

STALK A PUPPY (FREE!)

The next time you see a neighbor or local figure toting a brand new, clumsy-pawed puppy, don't merely admire from a distance. Take action, courting the puppy and puppy's owner as if you were a romantic paramour. Distinguish yourself from the pack by asking specific questions about the dog's breed, weight, and temperament. Consider carrying bits of savory bacon in a plastic baggy, which you can offer the puppy (consulting with the owner first, of course). Once you've forged a bond with both ends of the leash, you can then enjoy all of the vicarious thrills of puppy ownership without any of the tiresome house-training or all-night bark-a-thons. Soon you'll become a favorite figure in the park or on your block, at which point you can go in for the kill: offering your puppysitting services, where you'll have a whole weekend to spend cavorting and snuggling with the little guy.

THINK LIKE A PARISIAN SOCIALITE ($$$)

 You know who has cornered the market on happiness right now? A twenty-something baroness or male aristocrat rocking the Marais district of Paris. Try to emulate Maxime or Vivienne and adopt his or her *je ne sais quoi* glamour and carefree, proudly indulgent lifestyle. Here are nine pointers (because "ten" is just so bourgeois):

1. *Chocolate for Breakfast:* Yes, *pain au chocolate* and a double espresso are far more happiness-producing than a sad bowl of oatmeal and burned coffee. Start your day off with decadence! Also: your day now starts at 2 p.m.

2. *Suffer for Fashion:* For women, wear heels. At all times, as high as it gets. For men, try spectator shoes or vintage wing-tips. Throw together unexpected combinations, like knuckle rings and suspenders, or a Victorian-style jacket with latex leggings. Never look too dressed up, but rather exude devil-may-care street-chic whenever you leave the house. If this is too confusing, just wear black.

3. *Smell Good/Look Tousled:* Never leave home without putting on perfume or cologne. For tips on getting free perfume samples, see page 107 (Strategic Sampling). And while you should be freshly showered, don't overcomb or spend too much time styling—you want at all times to achieve a Brigitte Bardot bedhead or Jacques Charrier insouciance.

4. *Lunch—Now an All-Day Activity:* "Lunch" should consist primarily of white wine, paid for by someone richer and older than you. It should never be a time for discussing business or checking your iPhone. Instead reserve these precious midday

hours for flirting and casual, careless innuendo. Lunch should last from 3 p.m. to roughly 9 p.m.

5. *Love the Nightlife:* Only frequent establishments where people dance on tables. Cultivate a signature cocktail, something chic and simple with no gimmicky American name or sickly sweet aftertaste: Vodka soda with lots of lemon is a good start.

6. *Befriend a DJ:* You cannot think like a young Parisian social-ite without a celebrity DJ on speed dial. Even if you have to forcefully befriend or invent one, this is an absolute must.

7. *Cultivate a More Refined Playlist:* Ditch your played-out '80s mixes and lukewarm R&B and surrender to the au courant neotribal movement: Gang Gang Dance, Shapes Have Fangs, Blood on the Wall. This type of darkly creeping indie/low-fi techno gives you all the Euro, none of the trash.

8. *Develop an Obscurely Glamorous Side Hobby:* Develop a culturally superior hobby like making art videos or fashion styling, and when someone asks you what you do for a living, instead of "Account Manager," say that.

9. *Say Yes to Vices:* Be sure to indulge in all of them. Smoke, drink, dabble in drugs, wear fur, eat red meat, say un-PC things, scorn public transportation, and get rid of tiresome middle class hang-ups like "worrying," "employment," and "monogamy." C'est la vie!

(with thanks to Josephine de la Baume, actual Parisian socialite)

LAUGHING MATTERS (FREE!)

  When you laugh, you stretch muscles through-out your face and body, your pulse and blood pressure go up, and you breathe faster, sending more oxygen to your tissues. Laughter also dissolves stress, helps you relax, and boosts your immune system. Try two minutes a day of designated laughter and reap the benefits, both real and imagined. If you work in a particularly hushed office, you might want to reserve your "laugh break" for a solo trip in the elevator, or quick jaunt outside the building. If this is too inconvenient, try smiling instead. Cracking a big, broad smile during a particularly bad situation such as traffic, a stressful task, or an annoying conference call might make you look maniacal and scary, but you will be surprised how the act of smiling can trick your brain into thinking you're actually happy. It seems like cheating, but it isn't.

HAPPINESS HINT

Five Things to Laugh about (If You Can't Muster Genuine Hysterics on Your Own)

1. Rollerblading accident
2. Boardroom flatulence
3. Angry sock puppets
4. Amateur mimes
5. Famous comedy duos: Laurel and Hardy, Mel Brooks and Harvey Korman, Dan Aykroyd and John Belushi, Gene Wilder and Richard Pryor, David Spade and Chris Farley, Jeff Daniels and Jim Carrey, Harold and Kumar

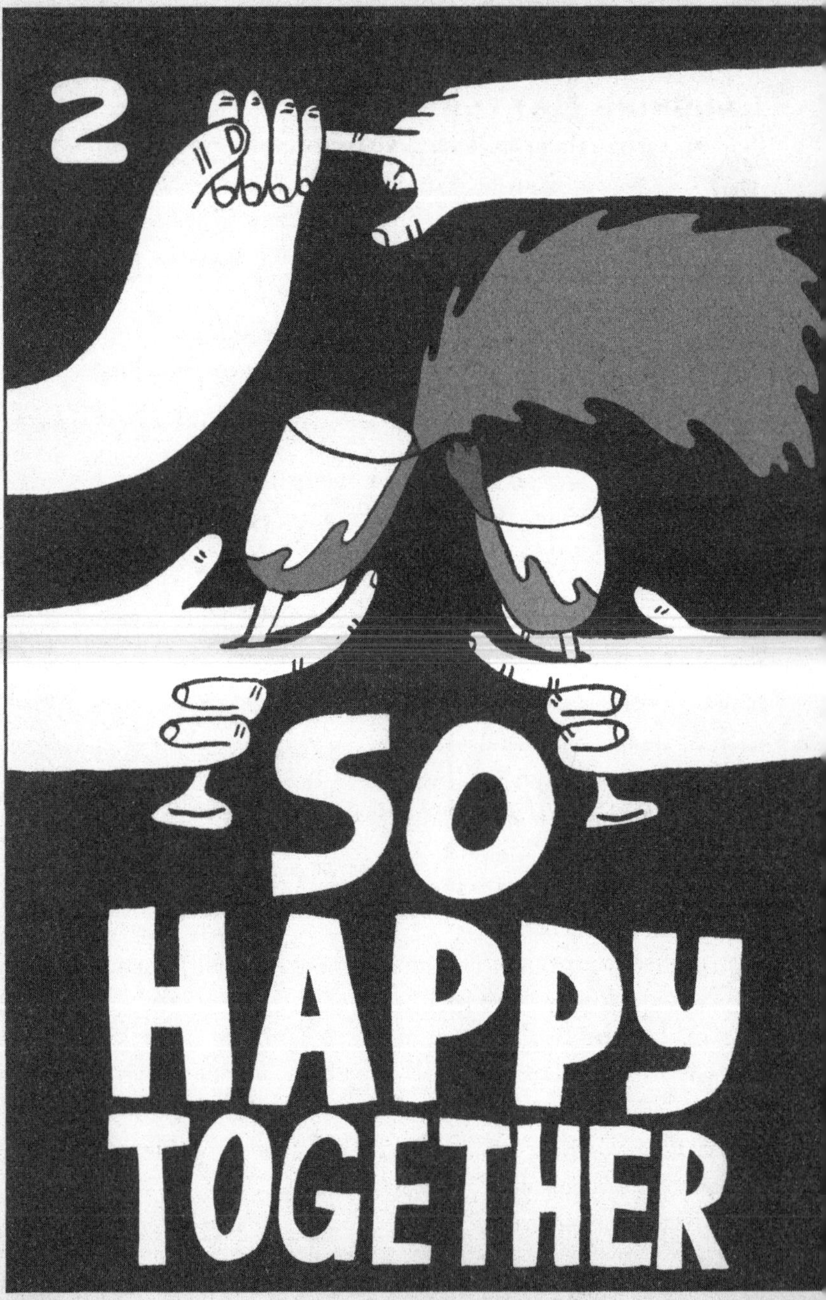
2
SO
HAPPY
TOGETHER

Good times best enjoyed en masse

*"Happiness is like a kiss.
You must share it to enjoy it."*

—BERNARD MELTZER

Studies show that happiness is contagious. Test this theory and spread the joy with a bevy of fun activities for groups of two or more.

BABY ANIMALS AND BELLINIS ($)

   Way back in our agrarian past, you could experience wildlife without the help of YouTube or the Discovery Channel. Now that you're broke, it's time to regain actual contact with our four-legged friends . . . yes, in person. Even the most cold-hearted and cynical will find it hard not to crack a smile or a subconscious "Oooh . . ." when confronted with fuzzy, lovable baby chicks or a tiny pony munching on hay. Combine this activity with the giddy combination of cheap prosecco and a splash of fresh peach puree and you officially have yourself a good time.

First, whip up a large quantity of Bellinis and place in a plastic container (like those outdoorsy water bottles that can supposedly withstand a drop from Yosemite's Half Dome). The container is usually tinted, which masks the carbonation and giveaway peach puree. You'll also look like you're the type of person who gets out in the wilderness, which will reduce suspicion. Next, go in search of unadulterated cuteness. Here are a few places you can frequent without looking creepy and/or menacing:

Pet Store Window Most cities or towns have a pet store that sells puppies, and displays them in the window for your impulse-buying needs. It's the perfect spot to ogle, sip, and argue over who's the pick of the litter. Note: do not buy any puppies, no matter how drunk you get.

State Fair This might involve a designated driver, as state fairs tend to be an hour or so away from where you live. Once you get there, you'll find an almost unending array of baby lambs, little chicks, itty bitty piglets, tiny goats, and other barnyard friends. This is also a good venue for your passionate vegan friend to make some new converts when you realize just where, exactly, all the cute animals are headed.

Dog Park Any afternoon spent at a dog-friendly park is all but guaranteed to produce results. Some parks even have specialized events like "Dachshund Sundays" or "Pug Wednesdays." Pick your favorite breed, sit back, and watch the pups frolic. If you wish to pet one, be sure to ask the owner if he or she is friendly and let the little guy sniff your hand first. Then, pet away. (But try not to let the owner smell your Bellini breath.)

Zoo Several zoos have a petting zoo area that hosts fuzzy friends, but don't neglect the polar bear lagoon or the lion's re-created Serengeti. Keep your eyes peeled, and the first person to spot a baby lion, tiger, or bear buys the next round.

Natural History Museum They might be stuffed (or extinct), but the baby animal contact high can be just as significant. Note: baby stegosaurus, baby woolly mammoth, baby pteranodon. Aww.

Local Lake or Reservoir There will be ducks galore. This is quite often a fantastic place to combine with your newfound benching hobby. Bring bread, and you'll soon feel like the popular kids on yearbook signing day.

BRING BACK GAME NIGHT (FREE!–$$)

 In the '50s and '60s, it was de rigueur to host friends every now and again for a night of bridge or backgammon. During these games, marital scores were settled, underhanded flirting was executed, midcentury politics was discussed, and many, many Lucky Strikes were smoked. Politely removing the bludgeoning cigarette haze from the equation, consider reviving the robust spirit of competitive, noncontact play and host a modern take on Game Night at your home, apartment, or after-hours office space.

Pimm's Cup Pictionary

Pictionary had its heyday during the hypercompetitive '80s, then lost favor in the '90s to more touchy-feely group games like

Taboo or smarty-pants ones like Scattergories, and disappeared entirely when Guitar Hero and Grand Theft Auto emerged. But whip up a batch of crisp, bittersweet Pimm's Cups, bust out the old Pictionary board, and you'll remember the agony and the ecstasy of this draw-to-win game. To up the stakes and make the game slightly more relevant, bring a blank set of index cards and have each team fill out category ideas for the opposing team. This way, you can rely on the very latest popular culture and inner-clique gossip to spice up an otherwise mild afternoon. Attempting, for example, to draw "couture jumpsuit," "Junot Diaz," or "graphic design whore," especially when buzzed on Pimm's Cup, can bring a whole new competitiveness to the game.

Hop Scotch

First, you need a piece of chalk and a low-traffic sidewalk. (This can also be played inside, with masking tape on the floor.) Mark up a classic hopscotch diagram with eight squares. Each player has a marker such as a stone, shell, bottlecap, quarter, etc.

- Toss your marker in the first square. Hop over square 1 (you must skip any square that has a marker in it) to square 2.
- Hop through the grid on one foot unless there are two squares side-by-side, where you jump landing with one foot in each square.
- Hop to the end, jump and turn around 180 degrees without leaving the grid, and hop back.
- Pause in square 2 to pick up the marker, and hop out.

Repeat these steps with square 2, square 3, and so on. You're "out" if:

- Your marker fails to land in the right square.
- You hop on a space that has a marker in it.
- You step on a line.
- You lose your balance when bending over to pick up the marker and put a second hand or foot down or hop outside the grid.
- You hop into a single space with both feet.

To spice up the game, you need a bottle of very good scotch. It must be single malt, it must come from Scotland, and it should be at least eighteen years old, although twelve will do in a pinch: Macallan, Glenlivet, Oban, Aberlour, Laphroaig, Balvenie. Split the cost equally among your group (you may need to recruit up to ten people). The goal here is that the participants of the game receive only a dram of sweet, delicious scotch if they manage to successfully traverse the hopscotch course without getting called out. In this way, the most skilled participants also end up getting the most inebriated, so the playing field evens out.

HAPPINESS HINT

The key to enjoying a fine scotch is how it's served. Always provide a glass of water and drinking straw to each participant. With your thumb, trap a drinking-straw's worth of water and deposit it into your glass of scotch. This helps open up the flavor (and makes it go down a bit smoother for the scotch novice). Don't serve a fine scotch on the rocks, as the ice will just freeze and dilute its flavors.

Connect Forties

One of the simpler and least athletic pastimes, all you need is an original Hasbro Connect Four game (a travel edition will also work) and two forty-ounce bottles of fine malt liquor. Choose your color, red or black, and dive in to this exciting vertical tic-tac-toe variant. The catch is, every time you successfully get four in a row and win, your opponent must swig their forty until you count to four—this can take up to 30 seconds. Another catch: whoever gets up to pee has to forfeit a turn. This makes for tense and exciting play!

Note: an offshoot of this game, Eighty Ounces To Freedom, should be attempted only by the very bored or the very stupid. The rules are as follows: two players sit on opposite ends of a couch. Each player has a forty-ounce duct-taped to each hand. The players must finish *both* forties without removing the tape. (Note: this both negates using the bathroom and seems to encourage projectile vomiting.) It's unlikely that either player will make it to the end of what will likely be two extremely lukewarm bottles of malt liquor without some sort of unsavory episode, so the point of the exercise is to take photos and post them online as soon as possible, because sharing this experience with the world is where the real happiness kicks in.

START SOMETHING ($–$$)

 Why not start a backyard wrestling league? Shoot your very own Super 8 horror film? Get a rockin' band together? Bring back the art of the 'zine? The problem with our new digital passivity is that we're losing the ability to connect, in person—and to collaborate on creative endeavors of dubious merit.

Sure, backyard wrestling may seem complicated, but you don't need a referee, bloodlust, or a large supply of crystal meth to faux-pummel each other while wearing ridiculous outfits. You just need a few good character names, well-padded performance gear, something resembling a ring (an Aerobed taken outdoors works wonders here), and basic (e.g., "no biting") ground rules.

The same goes with amateur filmmaking—all you need is a digital camera and a hastily written screenplay. If you decide to direct, everything should ideally move very fast—nothing kills the momentum like too much planning, and nobody cares about sticking to your meticulous shot list or getting the "right light." Write, cast, and shoot your horror film in one day for maximum enjoyment. If you're short on free talent, remember that having your cast play multiple characters with the aid of slapdash disguises will only heighten the entertainment value.

When deciding to start a band, realize that 90% of the task is deciding upon a cool name. You can hold weekly band meetings that consist entirely of good-natured sparring over the merits of "Captain Asstastic and the Star-Shit Troopers" versus the more genteel "Larry & Balchy." Over time, this activity will preclude all the labor, lyric writing, expensive equipment, rehearsing and performing of actually being in a band. But you should always make T-shirts, even if you never play a single gig.

And finally: print is only dead if we let it die. Give all the naysayers the proverbial ink-stained middle finger with this all-but-forgotten medium. All you need is an idea, a pen, typewriter, or computer, a stapler, proximity to Kinko's, and friends who will either contribute or read. When choosing your subject, think hard. But not too hard. Nobody wants to read your subatomic particles 'zine. Instead, think of something you really love (Mexican hip-hop, home brewing, horror films, Camaros, steak sandwiches, synthesizers, *The Hills*) or really hate (teacup poodles, Ugg boots, fake midcentury furniture, United Airlines, *The Hills*). Or commit yourself to a scorching backlash 'zine for a scintillating jump-the-shark read. Whether it's taxidermy, cynicism, skinny jeans, or Brandon Flowers, being over something before everyone else is just so satisfying (for example, the classic '94–'95 'zine *Die, Evan Dando, Die*). Assign your friends plum jobs like art director, managing editor, features editor, and beat reporter. As editor-in-chief, promote at your discretion and encourage both fierce competition and staff fraternization. Have a launch party with 'zine-scale amenities (think cherry Kool-Aid, pizza bites, Milwaukee's Best, and vinyl records). You may only publish one issue per year, ever, but it's fun, cheap, and expressive, and cooler and more retro-chic than blogging—and far easier than buckling down and writing that novel or screenplay.

DIY Karaoke (Free!–$)

Karaoke has become a national pastime, but the problem with frequenting karaoke bars (besides the hipsters, that is) is the sheer volume of cocktails required to provide the liquid courage necessary for taking the stage. In truth, you don't need overpriced watered-down sake, prerecorded rhythm sections, *or* dreamy digital montages of birds taking flight to rock the party. Nor do you need to invest in a fancy, next-generation digital karaoke machine from Brookstone. There are myriad online karaoke applications (try the karaokechannel.com) that give you access to hundreds of free songs (or, for a nominal monthly fee, literally *thousands* of songs). Hook your computer up to your stereo speakers, invest in a microphone, and build a small stage—filling shoe boxes with old books and stacking them is a foolproof trick. Then, invite your friends (or enemies) over for some ice-cold Sapporo and let the sonic magic begin.

SPYING, SNOOPING, AND OTHER "REALITY SHOWS" (FREE!)

 This much is true: either you or someone in your circle of friends has an excessively weird neighbor. Whether this person is filthy rich, sexually uninhibited, or known for employing unorthodox dance moves, there's something about them that draws a lingering, even morbid fascination. Throw a "reality show" surrounding this unsuspecting exhibitionist and place small wagers on things like how much the chandelier cost, how mighty his stamina is, or how many Double Stuf Oreos she can mow down in one sitting. A variant of this soiree is the "Weird Roommate Open House," wherein you invite your friends into your roommate's lair (when they're out, of course) and marvel at his or her strange possessions (water-bra, nunchucks), embarrassing CD selections (Technotronic: Pump Up the Jam!) and general bad taste (motivational posters, midget porn collection).

GROUP PARTY CRASHING (FREE!)

 "Cocktails and hors d'oeuvres will be served." That's really all the criteria needed to decide if a party is worth crashing. Of course, weddings are sure to provide both hot appetizers and ample cocktails, but potential hazards abound, from assigned seating to senile relatives talking your ear off. Try instead to look for openings—any time a museum, gallery, design store, boutique, or studio of any sort decides to throw open their doors after closing hours and serve room temperature but generally inoffensive chardonnay, you must be there. It's far more fun with friends, so go en masse. And don't shrink in a corner and look suspicious—in order to go undetected at an avant-garde event, you must be bold. Wear either all black or all neon (good for attracting cater-waiters), stand in a corner, puff your chest out slightly, and look imperious. Have an answer handy to the question, "How do you know the artist/designer/boutique owner?" A fail-safe answer is "we took a class together." Who knows. Maybe you did. Then shift the conversation to the present. "It's such brave work," you might say, or, "This is a stunning space. Who was the architect?" If you ask a question about an architect at an event such as this, you're usually in the clear. But try to refrain from stuffing every hors d'oeuvre in your mouth—a good rule of thumb is to refuse every other pass from a cater-waiter, even though you may need to physically restrain yourself from doing so.

JUST DO IT: SEX! (FREE!)

 Tonight, forget *American Idol*. Forsake your attempt to master Indian cuisine. Instead, try the ultimate stress reliever and happiness producer: sex. Studies show regular sexual activity lowers blood pressure, boosts immunity, and even raises self-esteem. You don't have to worry about what to wear. You don't have to spend a dime (hopefully). You don't need to be articulate, sophisticated, or even especially athletic, although the latter doesn't hurt. In order to make your sexual experience as enticing as possible, follow a few guidelines. Candles and mood music are fine and all, but what really makes things steamy is good personal grooming. Take a nice hot shower beforehand, and if you have a razor, go to town on areas not generally visible to the naked eye, but quite visible when you are naked. Apply perfume or cologne, but not in excess; your natural scent is always the most alluring. Have a glass of wine, but not the whole

bottle. And always be prepared: if you feel like doing something out of the ordinary, like a sexy striptease, try it in the mirror first to make sure that it is in fact sexy, and not unintentionally hilarious. Similarly, if you buy some sort of toy or outfit, give it a test run first. There is nothing worse than fumbling around for AA batteries in the kitchen drawer or needing the jaws of life to get out of a complex corset. Get things going with a short viewing of the type of website you aren't allowed to visit at work, and don't underestimate the power of a soundtrack: the dreamy, trippy early Bee Gees, gold standard Barry White, or the immortal crooner Ginuwine are all sure bets for sweet love.

HAPPINESS HINT

Dirty Talk Is Cheap!

Talking dirty to your partner is the easiest and most cost-effective way to get a rise out of them. If you do decide to heat things up with some colorful language, you must commit—immerse yourself as though you're an actor in an Oscar-worthy role. You might be shy or self-conscious about this at first, but practice makes perfect. Viewing the odd porn flick or picking up an erotic novel at the bookstore is a great way to cultivate new material. After all, variety is the spice of life. If you always say the same rote "Ride me big boy!" phrases, they will likely diminish in impact. Keep an open mind and don't self-censor—usually the first words that come into your head are the best. Here's a handy fill-in-the-filthy-blanks guide to get you started:

- Mmm, your _____ is so _____!
- It drives me crazy when you _____ my _____.
- I've never seen a _____ so _____ before!
- Yeah, _____ that _____!
- You're really turning me on, you _____ _____!
- C'mon, you _____, _____ my _____!
- Oh, _____! You're gonna _____ me _____!

Experiment, and most of all, have fun. And if you start laughing, it's OK, just start over!

STANDING ROOM ONLY (FREE!–$$)

You'd be surprised how many upscale cultural events have price breaks and discounts. These loopholes are ostensibly to give access to young, poor students, but aren't we all students of life? Most major museums, operas, ballet companies, symphonies, and lecture series have programs to accommodate the not-so-well-off. If you visit the San Francisco Museum of Modern Art on Thursday evenings, admission is half off, and on the first Tuesday of every month, admission is free! Chicago residents get a discount on visits to the Field Museum, just by showing proof of residence. The J. Paul Getty Museum in LA is *free* (although parking is $10 per car). And if you want to visit Lincoln Center in New York, the Metropolitan Opera offers Standing Room Only tickets for $15. This may seem like an uncomfortable way to see a three-and-a-half-hour performance of *Tristan und Isolde*, but the SRO section is actually quite plush, with velvet-covered arm rests. What's more, at intermission many opera goers who aren't sticking around for the second act will hand their tickets to the Standing Room attendant, who then gives them out (first come, first served), so you might wind up watching the rest of the performance in high style. On this note, if you are a real theater buff, many organizations have a volunteer usher program: with minimal labor you'll get to see dozens of free shows and enjoy the small bit of authority that a vest and tiny flashlight affords you.

Community theater is also an option for the culturally curious but cash-strapped. This experience is notable not for the show itself, but for the minute that you realize it's over. The euphoria and sense of giddy relief that follows a particularly brutal production of *Brigadoon* or *The Fantasticks* from the

Westport Dinner Theatre is something that no designer drug can replicate. These shows are usually very cheap and sometimes, at intermission, they serve refreshments. Usually it's a cash bar, but you'll find that a four-dollar plastic glass of Charles Shaw chardonnay or a fifty-cent glass of pink lemonade is like manna from heaven. Brace yourself for the second act by savoring each sip, spacing out, staring at the flyers for classical guitar lessons and pottery tours of Peru. Back in your folding chair, you may find yourself in a new state of mind, harboring an unexplainably powerful crush on one of the lustier cast members, or just letting your thoughts drift in the way they only do at the oral surgeon or Brazilian waxer. When you get that tingling in your bones that this bravura solo or crushing monologue may mean a conclusion to the proceedings and, at long last, you stand up to applaud, you are not just applauding the thespians onstage, but your ability to sit through two and a half hours of dramatic dreams deferred—and survive.

Add an extra element of danger and hang outside the back-stage door, where you can congratulate the players on their "powerful performance." You will hence be known as a sup-porter of the arts, and they will remember this comment for the rest of their ambitious but talent-free lives. Breathe the air outside and head out for the nightcap or ice cream cone that you now so richly deserve.

URBAN HIKING (FREE!)

For those who live in cities, hiking is a specific and ritualistic pastime. You round up some friends, put on perfor-mance-enhancing outerwear, pack a backpack with electrolyte-

balancing liquids, baggies of Kashi cereal, and possibly a joint, and hop in the car. Far outside the city limits, you stride through hill and dale, remarking on the air quality and how great it feels to "get outside and away from the city." But since when did "outside" and "city" become mutually exclusive? With the right footwear and the right attitude, a day on foot with friends in the metropolitan area of your choice will yield just as much unexpected majesty, healthful exercise, fresh air, and exposure to wildlife as that bitchin' sweet trail in the Ridgemount Headlands.

You'll need supplies such as sunglasses, fashionable walking shoes, and a camera for recording the trip. Don't get too hung-up on route planning; while it doesn't hurt to have a vague destination or goal, the urban hike is all about discovery and digression. Embrace all side streets and hidden shops. Sample vendor food and take a moment to listen to a street musician without cringing. Try to get close to a body of water at some point and take a *Karate Kid*–style posed photo or two. Be sure to stop at some faintly educational or cultural location (Korean art museum, Dutch pirate memorial, Jack London's house), read every plaque you come across, and contemplate what street names really mean. Instead of looking at distant vistas, look up the buildings, wonder about who built them, when, out of what, and why. Once you've embraced the secrets of your city with a sense of discovery and historical appreciation, you're free to drink the afternoon away in one of its many fine dive bars, which will no doubt be very happy to serve you.

Cheap Wine Tasting Party (free!–$)

Most of us have a go-to bottle of cheap wine that we enjoy perhaps a little too much. Under $10, it usually has a mildly embarrassing label with a duck or generic-looking chateaux on it, comes with a convenient screw cap (or in a box), and is readily available at major grocery stores and even the odd Rite Aid. You tend to hide this vintage when company comes over, instead serving a respectable $20 California cab or an exotic South African varietal to show off your taste and sophistication. Most people can barely tell the difference, which is why the cheap wine tasting party is such an ensured success. Everybody gets to share his or her guilty pleasure, and you can even include a voting element to spice things up, casting your choice for your favorite bargain Burgundy and anointing a King or Queen of Cheap Wine to whoever introduced it, fashioning a crown out of corks and toothpicks. Another crowd-pleasing element is to sneak in a really good bottle, invite your wine snob friends, and see if they can tell the difference.

TV/Cult Classic Movie Club (free!)

Book clubs are illuminating and lively ways to incite discussion and bond with your fellow literati, but some people have trouble getting behind the concept, due to lack of time or fear of judgmental fellow club members. A TV club may lack the erudition of a book club, but you'll avoid attracting those tiresome types who overprepare, arriving with highlighted passages and complex discussions of the novel's allegorical underbelly. Pick a TV show that is likely to start discussion: there are of course the high-end, high-concept cable series such as *Mad Men*, *The Wire*, and *Deadwood*, but you also have critically beloved but cancelled-before-their-time network offerings (*My So-Called Life*, *Arrested Development*, *Freaks and Geeks*). Don't neglect the lower-end of the TV trough either, e.g., reality shows, wife swaps, home makeovers, and, of course, *Intervention* and *Celebrity Rehab*. Another offshoot of this idea is a cult classic movie club, where at each meeting a cult favorite from the '70s, '80s, or '90s is viewed, with popcorn and attendant movie-watching accessories (beer, weed, Sour Patch Kids). The host gets to choose the film and subsequently defend it to armchair criticism.

REVIVE THE ARCADE ($)

If you live in a town with a locally owned pizza parlor, it's pretty likely that at some point in the '80s the owner invested in some newfangled video games to attract the younger crowd. Sure, they may have regretted this decision when the bleeps and bloops, requisite swear words, and roughhousing chased away the big-spending empty-nester clientele, but gradually the kids moved on to handheld devices, leaving these antiquated models and their quarter slots to languish next to the Hot Tamale dispenser that benefits muscular dystrophy. Why not revive the lost art of '80s graphics and the peculiar, mechanistic joys that only a joystick can bring? Head down to Sal's with a pocketful of quarters and see how quickly your reflexes return—how your fingers seem to remember how to throw a barrel, eat a cherry, and leap heroically across five lanes of two-dimensional traffic.

But don't just play for fun—play for keeps. Nothing spices

up a game like a friendly wager, and getting your friends to bet cold hard cash on your ability to reach the next level adds a whole new element of suspense to your afternoon fun. Start a Pac-Man tournament with your friends, choose teams, and devise a simple betting pool. Unlike college football, you can actually influence the outcome, spurring you to greater heights of ghost chasing and vine swinging.

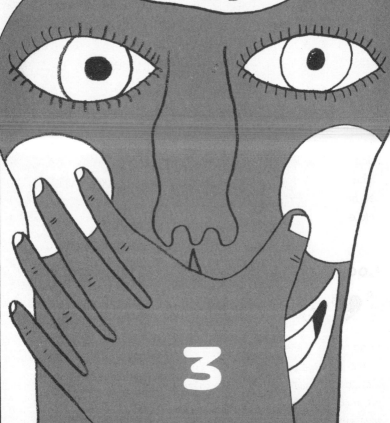

Artfully savoring the misfortune of others

"Happiness is an agreeable sensation, arising from contemplating the misery of others."

—AMBROSE BIERCE

"Schadenfruede" derives from the two German terms: Schaden (damage) and Freude (joy). In this chapter you'll see how far the mighty have fallen. And how mightily fun it is to enjoy their descent.

LOOK HOTTER THAN YOUR EX (FREE!)

Often, the real pleasures in life are intangible. Seeing a former flame in a bloated, tired, or sloppy state when you look fantastic is one of the fundamental sources of happiness in this world. The first part of this equation is strategic: by stealthily monitoring your ex's online activity, you can pinpoint the party or public gathering likely to reunite you with Mister or Miss Utterly Heartless. You may have to enlist a friend who is

Facebook friends with the ex, or who is on their Twitter feed, to be your eyes in the sky, but there is no shame in this. You would do it for them (and odds are at some point will).

Once you've found the right event, plan to arrive at "prime time," which is exactly one hour and fifty minutes after the projected start time. This makes you look busy and fun, but not rude, calculated, or blasé. Step two of the plan is to look incredible. Even just a week of going to the gym will improve your circulation and complexion, giving you that sought-after healthy glow that no amount of bronzer can replicate. On this note, if you choose to "get some sun" sans sun, at all costs avoid the orange Mystic Tan residue. Instead, invest in milder DIY products (Jergen's "Healthy Glow" or Guerlain's "Touch of Sun" lines are recommended). A new dress or outfit is good, the combination of a crash diet and too much hair product is not. Girls: don't be afraid of a little cleavage, but don't take it over the edge. You want to look refined and hot, not a *Rock of Love* casting tape reject. Men: get a haircut. Seriously. You have no idea the appeal of a new haircut. Remember when Carrie saw Aidan for the first time after they'd broken up and he'd cut his hair and lost the bad hippie jewelry? No? Don't worry, girls do, and they had the same reaction she did: Who is this handsome gent, and how can I get in his nonpatchwork pants?

STALK YOUR SUCCESSFUL FRIEND'S ONLINE PRESENCE (FREE!)

Gore Vidal once said, "Every time a friend succeeds, I die a little." It's a good thing he's too old for the Internet. The ability to track someone's ranking—whether it's their height on the great Google totem pole, their number of Facebook friends, or their passion project's progress on the Amazon charts—makes it nearly impossible not to become a sort of information-age fame voyeur. Do: take quiet satisfaction in their shifting fortunes. Do not: write a scathing review using a makeshift Yahoo address. That will not bring you happiness, only lingering e-guilt and brutal karmic payback once you attempt to do anything worthy of critical notice.

Important Subset: Smile: Your Ex's Novel Sucks

It was a love affair like no other. You supported him or her as they ground out the great American novel, listened to their rants, and nursed their insecurities. Then, the second they got a book deal, you were suddenly no longer necessary. They dumped you for someone younger and cuter and got their own place "with a study." As painful as these memories might be, keep in mind that the majority of debut novels are unreadable. And while there's a chance Oprah might anoint it to best-seller status, there's also a strong possibility that it will get tepid reviews (if any) and quickly move along to the half-off bin. Eagerly clip these tepid reviews, highlight the harshest lines, and save them to read on a rainy day.

AMASS SECRETS AS SOCIAL CAPITAL (FREE!)

A good, juicy secret is immune to economic fluctuations. It never devalues. If you are the type of person frequently referred to as a confidant, good listener, or trusted friend, you can, over time, accrue a mother lode of secret admissions, which you can then use to enhance your own popularity. A married friend is a frequenter of gay escorts? A business associate is cooking the books? A sanctimonious motherly acquaintance has a nefarious habit? Precious gossip, all.

Before proceeding, a qualifying term here is "flexible discretion." This means that you must know when to hold on to your secrets, and when to release them to your fascinated public. To get the maximum return on your investment, you must share the secret when demand is at its highest: a lull at a particularly stagnant cocktail party, a pregnant pause over coffee with an old friend, an obligatory work function such as office retreat or human resources conference are all intrigue-starved situations. The cocking of an eyebrow is an essential gesture, as is a hushed, yet confident tone. "I hear there's trouble in paradise," you might say, an oblique cliché that will only whet your audience's appetite. "What do you mean?" they'll implore. "Well, I really shouldn't," you say, decorously. "Please, we won't tell a soul," they'll cry. Pause reflectively, lean in conspiratorially, take a breath, and give just . . . one . . . juicy . . . detail. Then, check your cell phone and say you have to run. The more sordid a story, the longer you should take in revealing it, and in the meantime sit back and watch your social stock rise as your peers scramble to get the scoop out of you. Enjoy the awkward way they try to work up to the subject in subsequent encounters, "So . . . the other day . . . you were saying?" "Saying what?" "You know . . . about so-and-so." "Oh, yes, so-and-so . . . they're thinking about moving apartments, right?" "No . . . not that. The other thing." Then just stare at them piteously as they try to coax the secret out. Be wary of waiting too long, lest they find out the secret, or parts of it, from someone else, a predicament known as "gossip inflation."

FOCUS ON IMPERFECTIONS
(BUT NOT YOUR OWN) (FREE!)

  We all have a friend or two that seems to "have it all." They glide through life, perhaps with the benefit of a mighty trust fund. At ease in their perfect skin and tailored outfits, they charm everyone in their wake. Their relationships tend to be ones of sickening mutual adoration, their careers socially responsible and financially secure. They never fall victim to split ends, adult acne, bad breakups, hysterical crying jags, parking tickets, or the other indignities of modern life. Basically, they're perfect, and the only way you can feel the slightest bit of happiness in their presence is during the brief occasions, perhaps after a Maldives cruise, when they pack on a few pounds. Seeing their new, portly silhouette can be a moment of pleasure, giving you the chance to comment on how "healthy" they look. Augment this satisfaction by inviting them over and offering them an irresistible tray of soft imported cheeses, chocolate truffles, and scones with I Can't Believe It's Rich Creamy Butter.

SABOTAGE-AND-SODA HAPPY HOUR ($–$$)

  So your obsequious, ass-kissy, self-promoting, Cc-everyone coworker got a promotion. While you've toiled away unnoticed during late nights and early morning presentations, they roll in, take credit for the well-received ideas, and cannily shift blame for the misfires. They constantly have whispery closed-door discussions with the boss, who they refer to by a cheeky nickname and IM all day (you can tell this by the timing of laughter coming from the boss' office and your coworker's cube). Inevitably, you are forced to go out for celebratory cocktails to toast their rapid ascent up the corporate ladder. There are three essential steps for not only surviving this affair, but for basking in the joy of well-deserved sabotage.

1. *Prepare a backhand compliment speech.* Hoist a glass with a double-edged sentiment like, "For someone who never actually graduated from college, you have quite the noggin for business."

2. *Buy them a shot.* Not a drink. Not a beer. A shot—preferably something cheap and potent, yet sweet enough to encourage volume drinking, such as a lemon drop, a raspberry kamikaze, or a purple hooter.

3. *Encourage others to do the same.* The employee in question will likely feel uncomfortable turning down such congenial gestures. Think how fun it will be to witness his or her increasingly appalling and inappropriate behavior. Even better will be the next morning, when you swill your cup of coffee in front of their pale, sickly visage and inquire, "Are you feeling OK? You were pretty out of it last night."

ADVENTURES IN AMATEUR HACKING (FREE!)

 The digital age has created many wondrous and helpful modern conveniences. The wedding website is not one of them. We've all been directed to "jason-alisonwedding.com" to glean the location and ceremony details, only to be bludgeoned with long, self-serving descriptions of How They Met, perhaps augmented with video footage of the two of them walking through autumn foliage, or screen shots of the bride's and groom's Match.com profiles. (He is a religious listener of NPR! She works in PR! He loves Deerhoof! She enjoys "music"! Etc.) There will probably be a link to a registry and, in cases of extreme e-narcissism, an online poll where guests can help the lucky couple decide where their honeymoon should be (tour of Mayan temples, St. Barths, volunteering in Sub-Saharan Africa—you, humble wedding guest, can make your voice heard).

As irritating and sanctimonious as these websites can be, there is usually a "Comments" section, and that is where the real fun can be had. Disguise yourself with the subtly perceptible initials of a former flame of either bride or groom and simply write, "Why?" Or go to their online registry and secretly add a few weird or tasteless items. Always bookmark an overly elaborate wedding website, because months or years later, when he or she is complaining about the waning sex life, pressure to procreate, meddlesome in-laws, and mortgage costs, you can go back and revisit it, in all of its carefully worded, flatteringly Photoshopped glory, and smile smugly to yourself.

WATCH KARMA HAPPEN (FREE!)

 Making light of a serious global financial crisis is not always funny. Making light of individuals who flaunted their personal material gain in troubling and tacky ways is. We're pointing at you, Mr. Canary Yellow Stretch Hummer. And you, Mr. Swarovski Crystal–Bedecked Champagne Flute. And don't think our generic gin gimlet–eyed gaze has missed you, Mr. Pleated Khakis in Sag Harbor, Mr. Tiresomely Emulates the Cast of *Entourage*, Mr. Casually Mentions His Million-Dollar Bonus, and Mr. I Eat Kobe Beef Like It's Cracker Jack. Instead of, say, contributing to the culture, engaging in philanthropy, advancing the arts, or creating anything of value, these greedaholics used their sudden, staggering fortune to contribute to their coke stash, advance cataclysmic derivatives trades, and engage in horrific interior decorating. So, frankly, it's totally fine to smile and feel a warm glow spreading throughout your insides as you imagine some of these "players" lining up for job fairs at the midtown Sheraton or being forced to answer phones at a nameless accounting firm in White Plains. What's even more fun is to see their lifestyle—the bottle service that starts at fifteen hundred dollars a night, the black AmEx, the logo fabric—crumble and collapse, bit by bit, like a house of Louis Vuitton cards. But to fully savor this moment of well-deserved comeuppance, it's all about the comments you make when you see them in their new, reduced-bling lifestyle. "You look great, man!" "It must be such a relief to be out of the rat race!"

SEX TAPE SCREENING (FREE!)

 It is a rare and beautiful thing when someone in a position of power and authority is felled by the basest of human instincts: the desire to get naked, get it on, and get it all on digital camera. Whether this is a person you know or just someone orbiting around the pop culture cosmos, the urge to view the tape will be overwhelming. Make the most of this opportunity: don't just look furtively at your desk with the volume down. Invite friends and coworkers over to your place for a Sex Tape Screening. Get everyone nice and liquored-up (a specialty cocktail based on the film's participants, location, or theme is always appreciated—the One Night in Paris Veuve Cliquot or Pam-and-Tommy Buttery Nipple), and fire up the cinema-display screen for three and a half minutes of aghast gasps, giddy laughter, and eager shifting around on the sofa. Pass out review cards and have everyone rate the film and leave anonymous comments, then throw them all in a bowl and make each person read one that's not their own. This type of activity helps diffuse the weird vibes and voyeuristic guilt, and turns the whole event into a raucous, ribald celebration of human lust and folly.

DIVORCE PARTY! (FREE!)

 It takes a certain type of person to mark the dissolution of a lifelong commitment to love, honor, and cherish with an open bar and conga line. But if you happen to know such a person, why not sit back and enjoy the train wreck? Keep in mind the Divorce Party only elicits schadenfreude if the divorce in question is (1) someone you dislike, and (2) responsible for a ridiculously overblown wedding—otherwise you should spend the majority of the party cheering up the misguided host, and offering to set him or her up with a hot, successful friend of yours—fictional or otherwise.

Some tips for enjoying the moment: do not bring a gift. Do not go out of your way to bash the ex. If there are children, do not ask anything about their living arrangements. Do not join the conga line. And if the person is being obnoxious about the magnitude of their coming settlement, do not hesitate in asking who got "custody" of your wedding gift.

CALORIES OF CONTENTMENT

4

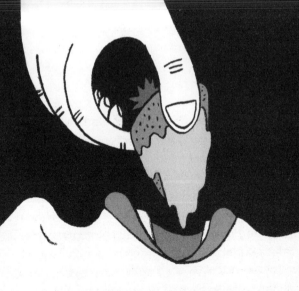

The joy of cooking
—and, of course, eating

> *"You can usually tell when I'm happy by the fact that I've gained weight."*
>
> —CHRISTY TURLINGTON

What we eat says a lot about who we are. Wouldn't you rather be "savory" and "saucy" than "carb-conscious" and "gluten-free"?

BE A HAPPY EPICURE (FREE!)

Does anyone really like a foodie—those serious connoisseurs who name-drop Matsutake mushrooms and Castelvetrano olives, genuflect before *Cooks Illustrated,* and break down the flavor profiles of a ten-course meal in ten seconds flat? While they might be skilled at posting eighteen-hundred-word treatises on Chowhound and experts at intimidating waiters, in truth a self-appointed foodie can be a terrific bore. This is not to say that you shouldn't listen to Michael Pollan or pay attention to what you eat and where it comes from, but a broader, more inclusive food philosophy that allows for the odd processed treat is likely to make you a happier person in the long run. Let's test that theory, shall we?

Quiz: Do You Need to Chill on Your Foodie Behavior?

1. Do you write reviews of restaurants that nobody pays for?
2. After dining at a four-star restaurant, do you demand a tour of the kitchen?
3. Do you have more than seven different types of olive oil in your home?
4. Do you use the term "fleur de sel" more than once a day?
5. Are you convinced that you should be the next TV food personality?
6. Do you correct your friends' pronunciation of terms such as "bruschetta," "sous vide," and "flan"?
7. Have you ever had a sex dream about Nigella Lawson, Anthony Bourdain, or Padma Lakshmi?

If you answered yes to more than four of these questions, you might be annoying your friends with your foodie behavior. Perhaps turn it down a notch, enjoy food without making it your religion, and remember the old proverb, "He who knows the most says the least." Or, in this case, "He who eats the best should pipe down already."

COMFORT FOOD ($–$$)

 The best cuisine is not all caviar and gold flakes. Many of us can truly relish the simpler dining plea-sures. Consider the emotional benefits of soulful comfort food. Make yourself a Comfort Food Pyramid, reconfiguring the classic FDA food pyramid to include staples of security and wallet-friendly indulgence:

Mac 'n Cheese Some people might tart this classic up with truffles and lobster, but a good bowl of Kraft Macaroni & Cheese ("in the blue box") will cure pretty much all modern ailments. For extra-cheesy goodness, top with a shredded hard cheese such as Gruyre, Manchego, or Asiago, then bake in the oven for 5–10 minutes.

Creamed Spinach For a brisk yet soothing, indulgent, and earthy side dish, create a "roux" out of flour and milk, then add the spinach and sauté until smooth. An ideal accompaniment to lean meats or even on its own. Great for hangovers, too.

Honey-Roasted Peanuts Roast your own peanuts in minutes. Your kitchen will smell terrific, and you get all of the sweet-salty snackiness without any of the unfortunate additives brought on by Mr. Peanut. Start with 2 cups peanuts (not raw). Preheat oven to 350 degrees. Heat 2 tablespoons butter with 3 tablespoons honey on stove top. Toss with peanuts, then spread on a cookie sheet and cook for 8–10 minutes until peanuts are golden brown. Remove, cool, sprinkle with salt, and serve with a crisp lager or citrusy soda.

Ribs (A Haiku)
O barbequed ribs
Fatty, falling off the bone
Messiness sublime

Yes, ribs are a one-way ticket to happiness. Any "secret recipe" for sauce is preferable to the bottled kind. In case you don't have significant barbequing ancestry, ask your friends and relatives for their favorite—your Texan friend will have an opinion. Bib is recommended, diet concerns are not.

Cookie Dough From the tube or made from scratch, it's hard to beat the grainy sweetness and sheer indulgence of the dough. (And cookie dough ice cream might just have been the greatest invention of the twentieth century, up there with the Model T and penicillin.)

Cured Meats Salami, prosciutto, and other cured meats have the savory, spicy, and soul-satisfying qualities one needs to be happy on a daily basis. A fun and easy party trick is to wrap your cured meat around a thinly sliced sliver of cheese. Hard cheeses such as Asiago or Manchego hold up best.

Mashed Potatoes Whether prepared for a holiday feast or made on the spur of the moment on a rainy Sunday evening, the silken, creamy, buttery, salty mashed potato deserves a lofty perch in the comfort food pyramid. If skinning and mashing a bushel of potatoes isn't within your motivational sphere, the straight-out-the-box kind is a compelling and cost-effective option.

Delivery Pizza What could be more happiness-provoking than the sound of the delivery guy's car idling in front of your house, a harbinger of a piping-hot $8.99 pizza? Stick with the most basic of toppings: pepperoni and mushrooms. If you want exotic, go with Hawaiian. Woe to the overeager or experimental pizza orderer who gambles on the "Mega Meat" pie from Domino's. This fast and easy (if fattening) delivery option will save you the trouble of menu planning, cooking, and dish-pan hands. Pair with a sporting event or fine film from the FX or Lifetime network for optimum enjoyment.

LET THERE BE CHOCOLATE ($–$$)

It's a medical fact: chocolate is good for you. Scientists say that a small bit of chocolate a day (preferably dark chocolate, which has less fat) is actually healthy! It lowers blood pressure and releases serotonin, which makes you happy. Here is more choco-for-thought:

- Cacao beans were so valuable in ancient Mexico that they were used as currency by the Mayan and Aztec civilizations. Yes, you could pay taxes in chocolate.
- Chocolate contains phenylethylamine (PEA), a natural substance that is reputed to stimulate the same reaction in the body as falling in love. So, if you're trying to seduce someone—send 'em chocolate!
- Chocolate was such as a prestigious luxury in the seventeenth and eighteenth centuries that the famously extravagant Louis XIV established a court position entitled Royal Chocolate Maker to the King.
- Chocolate syrup was used to represent blood in the famous shower scene in Alfred Hitchcock's *Psycho*.
- Hershey's Chocolate was called upon during the Persian Gulf War to create a chocolate bar that could withstand high temperatures. The "Desert Bars" were included in the soldier's daily rations.

Finally, when enjoying your daily dose of happiness-bringing chocolate, try to think in terms of quality versus scale:

one delicious Godiva truffle, savored slowly, is better than a one-pound bag of M&Ms wolfed down while scanning your ex's Facebook wall.

Hot Chocolate For One

(Recipe courtesy of Karletta Moniz, www.culinarymuse.com)

There's really no better pick-me-up than a cup of freshly made hot chocolate. Whip up a mug of this happiness ensuring elixir:

1 cup half-and-half
2 heaping teaspoons cocoa powder
1 teaspoon sugar
Pinch of salt

In a small bowl, stir together ¼ cup of the half-and-half, cocoa powder, sugar, and salt to form a smooth paste. Whisk in the remainder of the half-and-half. Place in a small saucepan and heat until it just reaches a simmer, stirring constantly. Best enjoyed in a heated mug.

GO TO STARBUCKS REHAB ($)

When did five-dollar coffee drinks become less of an indulgence and more of an everyday essential? Starbucks, bless their jittery hearts, has us all indoctrinated into their adult-sippy-cup culture. Many top executives simply can't function without their Starbucks beverage of choice, and all of us have fallen prey to the allure of their delicious seasonal beverages. But, following these simple steps, you can break free! Learn to make your own Vanilla Latte, Frappuccino, and plain old cup of coffee in the comfort of your own home, for less money, and without dealing with the surly and sleepy Starbucks barista who always forgets one or two components of your order:

✕ Vanilla Latte

2 cups water
3 ½ cups sugar
1 cup steamed milk
2 ½ tablespoons vanilla extract
½ cup espresso

To make vanilla syrup, bring 2 cups water to a boil. Slowly stir in 3 ½ cups sugar. As the sugar is dissolving, add vanilla extract. Once the sugar has dissolved completely, remove the pan from the heat. Allow it to cool and store it in the refrigerator in a well-sealed bottle (this is way more vanilla syrup than you will need, but you can save it for a rainy day). Make a double shot of espresso (½ cup), using an ultra-affordable Bialetti Moka Express Stovetop Espresso Maker ($29). Heat the milk in a small saucepan (or microwave for the impatient). Add a double shot of espresso to a 16-ounce cup. Add 2 tablespoons of vanilla syrup, followed by the steamed milk. Stir and enjoy with a pair of fuzzy pink slippers and stack of upscale home décor catalogs.

HAPPINESS HINT

Order eco-friendly 100% compostable hot cups and lids like Eco-Hot Cups (ecoproducts.com), decorate with your own creative branding, and take your cup of happiness to go.

✕ Frappuccino

Fresh ground coffee
1 ½ tablespoon granulated sugar
½ cup milk
1 cup ice

First, brew your coffee. Measure 2 tablespoons of ground coffee per 6-ounce cup in your coffee maker. Once the coffee is done brewing, place in your refrigerator until chilled. Then, pour 12 ounces of chilled coffee in a blender, add sugar, milk, and ice, and blend until the ice is crushed and the drink looks smooth. Pour into a frosty 16-ounce glass and enjoy on the porch with your feet up.

✕ A Great Cup of Coffee

Brewing a fantastic cup of coffee doesn't depend on luck or professional training; with the right information, anyone can be a celebrated brewmaster:

1. It's in the Beans

Select the freshest and highest-quality coffee beans. Never use preground or supermarket beans, which in many cases have been sitting around for weeks. The flavor sacrifice is just not worth the difference in price. Visit a specialty coffee purveyor and buy only what you need—remember, coffee beans are very perishable and can lose flavor in a matter of days.

2. Water Quality

Tap water is fine, but be sure it is cold and runs for a few moments first. Consider a water filtration device for a purer, smoother cup.

3. The Grind

To get the most flavor and freshness, grind your beans at home. Be sure to follow the grinding times for your type of brewing method.

4. Measure for Measure

Always measure the coffee to be used. Many people neglect this crucial part of the process and instead "eyeball it," throwing in an approximation of how much coffee to put in the machine. *One 6-ounce cup of coffee needs 2 tablespoons of coffee beans.* Ditch the giant, *Friends*-style coffee mug for a smaller, more compact, and stylish 6-ounce mug. Drinking less of a strong coffee is better than drinking more of a weak coffee.

5. Stir It Up

Always stir your coffee in the coffee pot before serving. This disperses the coffee evenly for more clarity, flavor, and consistency.

MAKE ICE MATTER ($)

  Ice is free, and with a small investment in clever, unorthodox ice trays you can liven up the most mundane beverages. With a quick Internet search, you can find ice cube trays shaped like lime wedges. Fill them with lime-flavored water and have them handy the next time a healthy glass of water seems too boring. Or purchase heart-shaped ice trays and fill them with grenadine-flavored water for a little romance in your water glass. For the pet lover, there are cat- and dog-shaped ice cubes (Yorkies and reclining tabby cats being the most prevalent). There are stars for the Fourth of July, dolphins and penguins for the aquatic/nature lover, and IKEA even has trays that yield cubes shaped like tiny bottles of wine for a drink-in-a-drink postmodern touch. But perhaps the winner of design-crowd ice cube tray development is Martin Zampach, a Russian designer who has created ice trays in the shape of old-school Tetris pieces (visit martin.zampach.com)—because sometimes a Tetris-shaped ice cube is the missing piece in the great happiness puzzle.

BROWN BAG IT ($)

So you've entered the workforce and have gotten happily accustomed to those miraculous direct-deposit checks every fourteen days. You know what "eats" away at all that hard-won income? Lunch. The average American spends $7–$10 a day on lunch alone, which adds up to $35–$50 a week or $1820–$5200 a year! It might seem pathetic to roll into your corner office with a paper lunch bag festooned with dinosaurs, but you'll have the last laugh during the next round of layoffs, when your egg salad–begotten nest egg kicks in.

A good tactic for a delicious bag lunch is layering. If you have a cold beverage (recommended), always place it at the bottom left of the bag. Then, place your sandwich horizontally next to it. This causes an automatic refrigeration effect. The next layer should be a cookie layer, followed by a fruit and snack—multigrain crackers with cheese are a good way to cut the crazed hunger in the afternoon. You can also keep the cookie to use as a precious barter item, which can be traded up, one transaction at a time, in order to secure yourself a prized office snack such as birthday cupcake or mini bottle of scotch. Some environmentally inclined folks will suggest a lunch box, but that might be taking it a bit too far, putting you in that category of "special" employees like the guy in the mailroom with the strange dent in his forehead.

PIGS IN A BLANKET ($–$$)

It's easy to dismiss this lovely Southern specialty as tired-out "white trash" kitsch from back in the early aughts where it was ironic instead of necessary to drink PBR. But whip up a bunch of these babies on a rainy Saturday afternoon, flip on a football game, and watch your friends frantically descend on them like so many Hungry Hungry Hippos.

The other brilliant thing about the P in a B is that they are almost ridiculously easy to make, especially if you're the type of person who doesn't flinch at premade dough or preprocessed hot dogs. Organically fed, locally farmed food is good and all, but sometimes Hickory Farms Lil' Smokies just feel right. Simply buy a can of Pillsbury croissants and a few packets of cocktail-size wieners. Cut each wedge of croissant dough in half, wrap each tiny pig in its doughy blanket, cook for 14–18 minutes, and serve with an array of spicy mustards. Best washed down with a frosty domestic beer, such as a Budweiser tallboy.

SEASONAL DELIGHTS THAT YOU SHOULD NEVER, EVER, DENY YOURSELF NO MATTER WHAT ($–$$)

Life is about choices: when to indulge and when to hold off. In certain situations, denying yourself the pleasures of the season, whatever that season may be, is less "watching your weight" than martyrish restraint. Embrace and indulge in all of the bounties of various holiday fare, secure in the knowledge that sentimental value trumps calorie counts every time:

Eggnog on Christmas Once dismissed as a musty turn-of-the-century holiday tradition akin to fruitcake and figgy pudding, the allure of the nog has been resuscitated in recent years. Perhaps it's pure nostalgia, or a renewed interest in sweet milky-flavored beverages brought on by the advent of chai, the frappe, and the Venti Caramel Macchiato. Whatever the case, don't deny yourself the deliciousness of holiday nog. Prepared with brandy, rum, or whiskey, served over ice with a sprinkling of nutmeg and cinnamon, you can use homemade or store-bought nog. Note the new development of "Lac-Nog," imitation nog for the lactose intolerant that is just as tasty as its dairy counterpart.

Latkes on Chanukah Just as you needn't be Christian to gorge on sugar cookies and candy canes, you don't have to be Jewish to enjoy this traditional crispy potato pancake. Served with sour cream or applesauce, this Hanukkah tradition is surprisingly easy to make:

Latkes

(Recipe courtesy of Alice Stern)

1 pound large potatoes, peeled
½ cup finely chopped onion
1 large egg, lightly beaten
2 tablespoons flour

½ teaspoon salt
½ to ¾ cup canola oil
(for frying)

Shred potatoes with a box grater or food processor shredding blade. Place the shredded potatoes in a kitchen towel and wring, extracting as much moisture as possible. In a medium bowl stir the potatoes, onion, egg, flour, and salt together. In a large heavy-bottomed skillet over medium-high heat, heat the oil until hot. Place large spoonfuls of the potato mixture into the hot oil, pressing down on them to form ¼-to ½-inch-thick patties. Brown on one side, turn and brown on the other. Let drain on paper towels. Place in a warm oven until all the batter is used. Serve hot with applesauce and a competitive game of dradle.

Champagne on New Year's Everyone wants to start the New Year afresh: with a personal commitment to get in shape, meet financial goals, learn a new language, and never, ever, drink again. Consuming your weight in Korbel the night before is a great way to spearhead the latter resolve. If there's ever a night to splurge, dance like a maniac, act inappropriate, text incoherently, and sloppily make out with some guy named Duane in the coat room, it's New Year's. Don't be boring and sip a beer or make yourself a discreet gin and tonic. It should be one glass of bubbly after another until it's time to move on to the next party. This way, you'll either kiss someone at midnight or be too drunk to care!

Russell Stover and Red Wine on Valentine's Day Whether single or in a relationship, February 14 will likely give you a decent amount of anxiety. Allay fears of perpetual singlehood or questionable partner choice with a heart-shaped box of drugstore chocolates and a decent bottle of Côtes du Rhône (French wine = trés romantic!). This is the one time when it's OK to sample a chocolate, recoil at its innards (Damn you, coconut! WTF, strawberry cordial?) and discreetly place it back in its designated chocolate slot for your partner's (or your, later, drunk) consumption.

Guinness and Reubens on St. Patrick's Day Green beer is for amateurs. Explore the bittersweet depths of an expertly poured Guinness at your neighborhood Irish bar this St. Patrick's Day. Don't be afraid of its thick consistency and room temperature tepidness—that's how it's supposed to look, feel, and taste. Surprisingly, a Guinness actually has fewer calories than it's seemingly leaner pilsner counterparts, so you can imbibe with less guilt. Savor your draught while filling your stomach with beer-buffering goodness in the form of a classic Reuben (corned beef, sauerkraut, swiss cheese, and Thousand Island, on rye).

Cadbury Creme Eggs on Easter Whoever invented this creamy, sugary, headache-inducing Easter treat should either be cheered or cursed. But there's something about the foil wrapping, the hard chocolate shell, and the seductively smooth egg-colored innards that lets your inner child have a sugar spaz-out, and what's more happiness-inducing than that?

Hot Dogs and Draft Beer on Opening Day Play Ball! Many people find our national pastime mind-numbingly boring, but those people are ignoring the transformative effects of a tall cup of frosty ballpark brew and a foot-long hot dog festooned with squeeze-pump ketchup and relish from a communal trough. The customary food and drink of the ballpark should be enough to allay anyone's fears of yet another pitching change, scoreless inning, or "How could it only be the top of the fourth when we've been here for two hours already?" freak-out. Peanuts, Cracker Jack, and the unsung hero, chocolate malt, are other important components to a perfect day at the ballpark.

Apple Pie on the Fourth of July It seems like a cliché, but apple pie really is better on the Fourth, served à la mode, on a red-checkered tablecloth, out in the backyard or by the lake with a sweet breeze blowing in the July heat. If none of this is even remotely in your grasp, consider a McDonald's Apple Pie, a walk to the public park, and purchase of cut-rate bottle rockets from the local bodega as a substitute.

Roasted Pumpkin Seeds, Mulled Cider, and Mini Snickers on Halloween Halloween is pretty much the greatest holiday ever invented. Kids get to eat candy all day and dress and act like ghosts, superheroes, sports stars, and popular animated characters. Adults get to do the same, only dressing and acting like sexually promiscuous versions of themselves. Everybody wins. Whether you're expecting trick-or-treaters or hosting an adult shindig, nothing says Halloween like roasted pumpkin seeds, with the added benefit that one must procure and carve a pumpkin to enjoy them. Simply pull out the goop and separate as many seeds as you can, clean in a strainer and place on foil on a baking sheet, sprinkle with salt and a bit of olive oil, and cook for 20 minutes or until they start to smell really good. Serve with mulled cider (see below) and mini Snickers and you'll have the most spooktacular cocktail party buffet in town.

HAPPINESS HINT

Making Mulled Cider

To make mulled cider, it's all about the spices. First, procure 2 quarts of fresh cider from the supermarket. Then place 1 teaspoon whole allspice, 1 teaspoon whole cloves, and 3 cinnamon sticks into a cheesecloth (a coffee filter will do in a pinch) and secure with a twist-tie or piece of ribbon. Combine ½ cup brown sugar, a dash of salt, and cider in a large pot. Bring to boil over medium heat, and throw in your spice ball. Cover and simmer all evening. For extra festivity, put a cinnamon stick in each mug as a flavorful take on a swizzle stick.

Pumpkin Pie on Thanksgiving Thanksgiving is a socially sanctioned excuse to stuff yourself. Like the proverbial bird, you should be so full of stuffing, mashed potatoes, and cranberry sauce (the turkey is almost an afterthought), that you can't possibly partake of a piece of pumpkin pie. But you can—and should! Know that all of these calories represent a mere blip on your annual intake, and even if it feels as if you consumed three pounds of food, you have not actually gained three pounds. A hearty, post-Thanksgiving walk to the video store may help revive you, as will shouting at the football game and dealing with the familial tensions that naturally arise during all holidays.

Be sure to watch for the presidential pardon of the turkey each year. A tradition dating back to Harry Truman's presidency in 1947, each year the president pardons one Turkey (and one understudy). Past birds include "Flyer" and "Fryer," "Pecan" and "Pumpkin," "Marshmallow" and "Yam," . . . you get the picture. The birds stay in the Willard Intercontinental Hotel two blocks from the White House, with room service, a gourmet meal prepared by the executive chef, and minibar stocked with Wild Turkey. Then the lucky bird gets to fly first-class to Los Angeles, where he serves as Grand Marshall of the Thanksgiving Day Parade in Disneyland. The turkey spends the rest of his days in safety, in a turkey sanctuary, far from the chopping block. Sure, we Americans have our share of problems, but you sort of have to love a country that does this with a straight face.

Birthday Cake on Your Birthday Hurray, it's your birthday! So much to celebrate: you're a year older, you need contact lenses, your back hurts, and your hangovers seem to last for three days. At least there's cake . . . sweet, delicious cake. Now is not the time to worry about your waistline; instead, demand a corner piece *and* seconds. If you're forced to have an awkward water cooler or conference room at-work birthday with a sad sheet cake provided by the HR lady, lighten the mood with anecdotes about your birthday's past (the twenty-first is always a good memory to revisit) and, in order to avoid awkward cursory invitations to coworkers to "come help you celebrate," simply announce that your best friend or significant other has planned something and that "it's a surprise."

FOUR-STAR FOOD, TWO-STAR PRICES ($$–$$$)

 Lying is bad, and does not make you happy. However, smudging the truth a bit is the American way. Heighten your social profile when dining at fancy restaurants and you'll often get better treatment, and extra freebies like an unexpected cheese course or a tiny cup of delicious summer squash puree as an amuse bouche. It all starts with the reservation. There are many ways to be treated like a king at culinary institutions. Restaurateurs love a wealthy foreign tourist, so when you call to make your reservation, affect an accent. Italian or British will do if French or German are too difficult (do not attempt Icelandic). Additionally, many restaurants now take reservations by email. Don't be a sucker and send your request to the generic reservation email address. Instead find the general manager's email and write a short, cordial email identifying yourself as a "food blogger" and request any "high-res" images that you might post to your site. If you don't already have a food blog, now is the perfect time to start. Blogspot.com is extremely easy to navigate, and you can record the highlights of your meal in glowing

HAPPINESS HINT

Courting the Comp

Occasionally—very occasionally—the management will pay for all or part of your meal. The reasons for this vary. Perhaps you convinced them you are important, or maybe they just found your presence particularly winning and an asset to the dining room. In the industry, such freebies are known as "comps"—complimentary food, beverage, dessert, or sometimes, thank your lucky stars, all three. Do keep in mind that just because the meal was free does not mean you shouldn't tip the waiter or waitress who served it to you. Always tip on the entire amount of the check. When there is no check, politely ask them to ring you up for a cup of coffee and then add 20% of your total bill on the gratuity line. Then you sign, smile contentedly, and leave.

detail, which, no doubt, will be chock-full of special treatment and obsequious service. Finally, calling ahead and identifying yourself as your own personal assistant never fails to give you that extra edge that transforms a cramped back-of-the-house center banquette two-top into a prime booth near the harpist.

BARSTOOL CUISINE ($$)

If you want to sample the famed menu of a culinary hero but cannot summon the scratch, dining at the bar is a time-honored tradition for the gustatory voyeur. Order a glass of wine. To earn the bartender/server's respect, don't ask for a plain old "house red"—specify something just-this-side of obscure such as Viognier or Sancerre. Then ask for a menu and peruse the appetizers. Order the one that looks the heartiest and most elaborate (look for quail egg, seaweed reduction, or house-brined anything), and you can tell all your friends you had dinner at Thomas Keller's latest and report that it was either divine or no great shakes. Either is equally satisfying. Dining at the bar is also a great way to meet people if you are single. Conversations come freely and easily, and there's no overt pressure or singles-bar desperation. Just be sure to have a book or magazine handy and an exit strategy in place in case your new companion becomes overbearing.

BAKE YOUR OWN BREAD ($)

This might seem like an extreme measure, but making your own bread is a satisfying and self-esteem-boosting domestic activity. It doesn't take much actual culinary skill other than patience, and you'll find the kneading portion of the recipe can envelop you in a Zen-like calm. And, when the bread rises, you'll feel a near-biblical sense of accomplishment. Also: your home will smell good for days. As if you "knead" another reason to jump on the bread wagon, it's fun to be at home, working on this hearty and wholesome project, as opposed to being outside, where you're far more likely to spend money and get into trouble:

✖ Wholesome Whole Wheat Bread (makes two or more loaves)

(Recipe courtesy of Amy Olsson)

2 envelopes of dry yeast, placed in ¼ cup lukewarm water with a little sugar
1 quart lukewarm water
⅓ cup brown sugar or 1 ½ tablespoons molasses
2 ½ teaspoons salt
2 cups whole wheat flour

¼ cup wheat germ
⅓ cup shortening (melted butter)
A little more than 2 cups bread flour
More white flour (another 2 cups or so)

Stir together everything except the additional white flour and let stand in a warm place for about an hour. Add more white flour until stiff, knead, and let rise in a warm place for about an hour. Push down and put into pans. Let rise again. Bake at 450 degrees for 15 minutes, then reduce to 350 degrees and bake another 1 to 1 ½ hours more.

RAVENOUS RATIONALIZING (FREE!)

Dieting is a grim existence, and not one that usually leads to excessive bouts of happiness. But pure gluttony isn't the best route to happiness, either. The best option is discovering foods that offer guilty-pleasure qualities while also providing you with hidden health benefits and, yes,

Happiness on $10 a Day

weight-loss assistance! Just knowing (select) facts about what you (be honest) were going to eat anyway can be an instant mood booster.

Steak The argument over red meat still rages in many health circles, but by the numbers a lean cut of beef has about the same amount of saturated fat as a skinless chicken breast. It's also chock-full of protein, which helps you feel full and makes you less prone to crazy late-night snacking. Stick with extra-lean cuts like T-bone or sirloin tip and try not to pair your steak with too many fat-laden accessories. Instead of cheesy mashed potatoes, try a baked potato with low-fat sour cream and fresh chives (or just eat the cheesy mashed potatoes and go to the gym tomorrow.)

Spaghetti You could swear off pasta, only to have carb-withdrawal drive you to a regrettable binge at your local Olive Garden. Instead of avoiding, switch to whole-grain pasta. Eating whole grains rather than refined ones can help burn belly fat. Just skip the Alfredo sauce and instead opt for fresh tomato and basil or a delicious—and affordable—canned red sauce. Prego!

Nuts Nuts are indeed high in fat, but it's the good (unsaturated) kind. They are also protein-rich and fiber-friendly, so while you might get a few grams more fat when partaking, it can help control sugar cravings later. Whole almonds are also a good source of Vitamin A and D and can be kept around the house or on your desk when the vending machine sings its 4 p.m. Nestle's Crunch siren song.

Cheese One theory (perhaps posed by a cheese-loving MD) is that the body burns more fat when it gets enough calcium, so cheese, yogurt, and milk can actually contribute to weight loss. While a diet of 24/7 Camembert probably isn't your healthiest option, don't throw cheese under the bus. Cheese in moderation, especially when served with fruit, can be a healthy, happy snack.

Red Wine The jury is in: a glass (or two) of red wine a day is good for your health and your outlook. Red wine contains antioxidants, which are like little magical elves that help thwart free radical damage at the cellular level. Thus, moderate red wine consumption can help prevent certain cancers and heart disease, and can even help lower your cholesterol. Salud!

Coffee Recent studies prove that drinking one to three cups of coffee a day can help lower your risk of Type 2 diabetes, colon cancer, and Parkinson's disease. In an unscientific study conducted by the author, one to three cups of coffee a day also tends to make you more popular around the office and can restore your will to live after a particularly late night.

BE A SNACK SOMMELIER (FREE!)

 Most food favorites go better when paired with a specific beverage. Oreos and milk, coffee and doughnuts, gin and regret. In time, you can become as sharp and intuitive as a wine sommelier, versed in the most rarefied pairings that heighten any culinary experience, no matter how humble. Your friends will also be happy to help you test out your latest combinations. Here are a few food and drink matches made in heaven to get your started:

Peanut butter brownies paired with whiskey sours

Shrimp tacos paired with watermelon aqua fresca

Mint chocolate chip ice cream paired with Bailey's

Peach cobbler paired with champagne

Pepperoni slice paired with root beer (pitcher preferred)

Lobster roll paired with Smuttynose Farmhouse Ale

Guacamole paired with fresh lime margarita and rock salt

Cheeseburger sliders paired with fountain Coca-Cola

Vending machine pretzels paired with cheap German beer

Fried chicken paired with strawberry milk shake

Trader Joe's crab cakes paired with screw-top sauvignon blanc

Entenmann's chocolate doughnut paired with black coffee

Twix bar paired with Diet Sprite and a dash of grenadine

HERB GARDENS ($–$$)

 So easy, so low-maintenance, and you'll look so culinary and hip when friends come over. Picture yourself chatting about art or cinema, pausing to extinguish your hand-rolled cigarette, then nipping out to the window box to snap up some fresh basil for the pomodoro sauce. Sophisticated and sustainable! The six herbs that are basically idiot-proof are as follows: parsley, thyme, coriander, basil, dill, and sage. You can buy a kit or head to your local home and garden center and assemble the perfect growing environment, including a gardening tray, soil or peat moss, and, of course, the seeds. Water thrice weekly (do not over-water). Some believe that a little bit of sugar in the water helps the plants nourish themselves and grow, although it could just give them a momentary sugar high. Of course, you could also augment your happiness and addle your consciousness by planting an entirely different sort of "herb" garden—we certainly don't condone it, but there are countless guides to this on your friendly neighborhood Internet.

THE DEVIL WEARS MAYO ($)

 The ultimate throwback party favorite. Keep in mind that balance is everything, in life, and in deviled eggs. Too much accessorizing and you have a fussy, overspiced mess; too little and you have a bland and unappetizing snack of atonement. As long as you get the ratio of mayo to yolk down, you can then take greater leaps, experimenting with flavors and ingredients. Bonus: eggs are really cheap!

✗ Classic Deviled Eggs

6 eggs
¼ cup light mayonnaise
½ teaspoon Dijon mustard

⅛ teaspoon salt
¼ teaspoon pepper
Dill for garnish

Place eggs in large saucepan. Add enough cold water to cover. Bring to simmer over high heat. Reduce heat to low, and simmer gently 5 minutes. Remove from heat, cover, and let stand 10 minutes. Drain eggs; cover with ice and water and let stand until cold. Peel and cut lengthwise. Remove the yolks and place in a small bowl, adding mayo, mustard, salt, and pepper. Mix thoroughly, then fill the empty egg white with the filling. Garnish with dill or paprika, cover with plastic wrap and refrigerate before serving.

Simple, right? And, you can spice up this egg-boiling template with some Latin flavor in this *muy picante* variant:

✗ Chipotle Deviled Eggs

6 hard-boiled eggs, shelled, sliced, yolk and whites separated
¼ cup mayonnaise
2 teaspoons finely chopped canned chipotle chilies
      (available at specialty food stores or Latin markets)
12 fresh cilantro leaves (to garnish)

(Recipe courtesy of Rick Rodgers, www.rickrodgers.com)

HAPPINESS HINT

Perusing your town's Latino market can be intimidating *unless* you have an easily attainable goal, such as procuring a can of common chipotle chilies. You won't have to haggle or speak Spanish, and you might pick up cool finds like vibrant-patterned fabric for use as festive tablecloths, cheap glassware, and votives galore.

THE BEST LEMONADE RECIPE EVER ($)

"When life gives you lemons, make lemonade." We've all heard this shopworn aphorism, and instead of cheering us up, it just seems to say, "Looks like you failed again!" Adding insult to injury, most people don't actually know how to make lemonade, thereby intensifying the sense of helplessness and defeat. Follow these easy lemonade-making steps the next time circumstances get you down, and feel a small bit of triumph that, while life's proverbial lemons can crush your dreams and spirit, life's literal ones can make a delicious, refreshing treat. Be sure to serve in a large pitcher with plenty of ice on a summer's day. A good, worn-in stirring spoon and rocking chair are also recommended.

✗ Perfect Goodtimes Porch-Sippin' Summertime Lemonade

6 *fresh* lemons
1 cup sugar
1 cup water
4 cups cold water

Use a juicer to extract the juice from the lemons, enough for 1 ¼ cups of juice. Make a simple syrup by heating the sugar and water in a saucepan until the sugar dissolves completely. Add the juice and the sugar water to a pitcher. Add 4 cups of cold water to dilute. Refrigerate 30 to 40 minutes. Serve with ice, sliced lemons, and folksy wisdom. And if you have the entrepreneurial spirit, there is nothing wrong with opening up a lemonade stand as an adult. Just be sure to check the market price for a Dixie cup of lemonade (currently 50 cents) and leave a tip jar for amassing untold amounts of "pity change."

5

SELFISH SELFLESSNESS

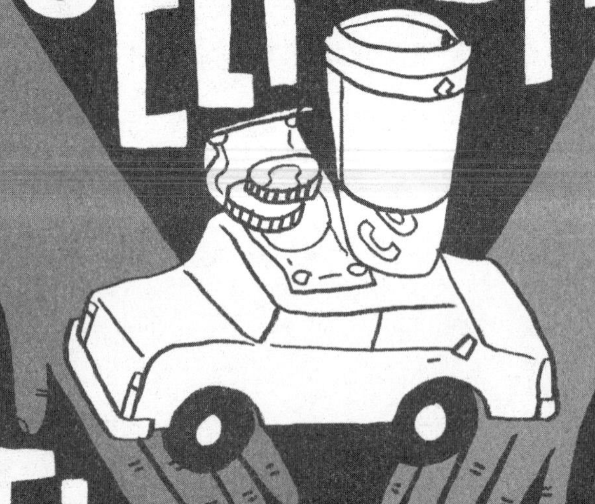

Good deeds that make you feel great

> *"To be without some of the things you want is an indispensable part of happiness."*
>
> —BERTRAND RUSSELL

Aesop famously said, "No act of kindness, no matter how small, is ever wasted." Whether tossing change to a marginally talented street musician or affixing a donor sticker to your driver's license, you can make a difference, without troublesome life-altering sacrifices.

FREELANCE BABYSITTING (FREE!)

 Having a child is the most rewarding, fulfilling, soul-enriching gift on this earth. It's also a tedious, libido-destroying nightmare. Offer your babysitting services for the beleaguered parents in your life—gratis. Let them enjoy a night on the town, free of their diaper genie, and you'll get to see what's going on in the world of CGI cartoons, play video

games without shame, and teach the kids colorful new terminology that is sure to surprise and delight their parents later. Another bonus: little kids tend to fall asleep around 7 p.m., so you can kick back, watch cable, eat popsicles, order pizza, snoop around the house, and bask in the warm glow of your goodwill. Do: watch where the kids roam, have a list of emergency contacts handy, make cookies out of tube-dough, challenge them to a board game, and construct a paper scepter and crown for the winner. Do not: fall asleep on the job, order pay-per-view movies (unless instructed otherwise), invite your significant other over, raid the liquor cabinet, or use the computer without erasing your history.

GIVE BLOOD . . . GET COOKIES (FREE!)

When you donate blood, you walk away with a host of happiness-providing things: the knowledge that you have potentially saved up to three lives, free cookies, an "I Gave Blood" sticker that will endear you to strangers, a faintly badass bandage on your underarm and a not unpleasant woozy feeling that lasts throughout the afternoon. You can get out of annoying meetings or conference calls with the totally valid excuse that "I gave blood this afternoon, and I'm just feeling a little lightheaded. I'd better sit this one out!" Everyone will silently, audibly, or begrudgingly commend you for your altruism—especially the boss who is about one steak sandwich away from heart failure. Some people actually get cash for donating blood, but that is not the point here. Once you start auctioning off your bodily fluids you've likely broken some sort of moral and social barrier that will bum you out for years to come.

WALK A QUARTER MARATHON (FREE!)

 Charity takes many forms. It could be a grand gesture, a significant financial outlay, or a deep personal sacrifice. Or it can just be a devotion to a cause, a minor physical achievement, and some group emails. This type of "microcharity" can really get results, if you're a little bit creative and not too preachy.

Pick a cause that is near and dear to your heart. Can't think of one? Here's a random sampling: cancer research, AIDS research, multiple sclerosis, Alzheimer's, and Animal Rescue. Sadly, one member of this "Big Five" has probably affected someone in your life. Propose a personal challenge and recruit friends to donate money via email or through one of the many social networking sites currently available. It helps if you're able to make the request both heartfelt and self-deprecating, as sometimes people get put off by the high achievements of others. Start by figuring out a character flaw. Are you lazy? Propose that you walk or run a quarter marathon (six and a half miles). Fashion a logo and entry number for yourself and have friends take photos of your triumph on the big day, posting them on your site. Are you attractive yet prudish? Say you'll pose in your underwear in public during rush hour if your donation goals are met. Do you have a fear of something—flying, sharks, old people? Announce your goal to conquer this fear, hopping aboard a 737, swimming with sharks in South Africa, or volunteering to teach improv comedy at an old folks' home. In this way, you'll not only raise money for the charity of your choice, but also perhaps conquer a fear and inspire people to embark on their own microcharity.

BE A ROLE MODEL (FREE!)

Kids en masse can be chaotic, stinky, and loud, but kids one-on-one can be attentive, sweet, and loyal. No matter where you live, there is likely a mentorship opportunity, whether Big Brothers Big Sisters or an after-school literacy program.

This may sound like a big commitment, but there are a few incentives beyond making a difference in a child's life. First of all, it's a great self-esteem boost. This kid is likely going to think you are way cooler than you actually are. Encourage this. Show him your cell phone or reference your private bedroom or ability to buy candy any time you want. And kids are often very good about solving life's more complex problems. Don't hold back—talk to them about your listless boyfriend or shady girlfriend, grad school confusion, or monetary woes. They usually will have a few no-BS, common-sense solutions that make all those hours in therapy seem like a self-indulgent waste. "If he doesn't want his mom and dad to meet you, why do you want to be his girlfriend?" Good question, kid. "Why would you *pay* to go to school?" Exactly. Also, helping a fourth grader with his or her homework is the perfect way to feel intellectually intact. And when that little sucker actually seems to have learned something from you, whether it's the point of verbs in sentences or the existence of Native Americans in his or her home state, prepare yourself for an unmistakable heartwarming glow.

SERVE UP A BOWL OF PERSPECTIVE (FREE!)

The author would never go so far as saying that a soup kitchen is a happy place, because then she would be outright lying. But, should you volunteer to help prepare food for the homeless and the downtrodden, especially during holidays or in inclement weather, you might stumble upon some intriguing revelations that will, over time, increase your happiness. Take the humbling factor of the task. Modern life, with all its shiny technological trappings, flattering social networking profiles, and painstakingly branded entertainment, has us pretty convinced that we are each very, very important. Doing good on any scale helps you even out that overinflated assumption. There's something about a task like making eighteen trays of cornbread or slicing five hundred strawberries that places your life in perspective. Doing charity strips you of your carefully crafted identity—the debonair wisecracker, the sweet spacey ingénue—hands you an apron and asks only that you do your part. You don't have to be "creative" or "modern," or "think outside the box," you needn't be a "tastemaker," an "icon," or a "successful person"—just chop the damn strawberries. In this way, you get to face your own limitations, see how good you have it comparatively, and feel altruistic, a mighty triad of well-earned self-awareness and, yes, happiness.

BE A VEGETARIAN FOR ONE WEEK (FREE!)

You might be a dyed-in-the-wool meat-and-potatoes person, someone who considers venison a snack food. The very thought of a tofu lifestyle might make the wood-paneled steakhouse of your soul burst into flames. And that's OK. But wouldn't it be interesting to see if you can live without meat for a week . . . and actually enjoy yourself? There are, of course, many ethical, political, and nutritionist arguments to be made both for and against meat consumption. There are burger-chomping ignoramuses that don't value or understand how the food choices they make are wasteful or potentially damaging to the ecosystem, just as there are some sanctimonious vegan types that also do their darnedness to take the happiness out of every meal. But a week of doing a little research and making a slight adjustment in your diet will give you intimate knowledge of the life of a peaceful veggie lover and a broader perspective of your place in the food chain. You'll be surprised at how much cheaper entrees are when they are not composed of grass-fed anything. You'll be dazzled by the delicious variety of Mexican food items that can be had sans *carne asada*, and amazed at how much lighter your step and your cholesterol levels will seem after a week of abstaining from "anything with eyeballs." Another bonus: pizza. Lots of pizza.

TIP AND OVERTIP ($–$$)

As anyone who has ever worked in the service industry knows, tipping can be a cruel mistress. Some flush and flashy patrons will leave a meager 10% on a filet mignon, while seemingly prudent suburban aunt-types will throw down 25% on their patty melt. It's a dicey proposition to base your income on the generosity of drunken strangers. What's more, diners' standards seem to have skyrocketed in recent years. We used to be pleased when a waiter wasn't outright rude, but now we want to be coddled, flattered, and amused. Remember that

"TIP" used to stand for "To Insure Promptness." Now it's more like "To Insure Polite, Charming, Knowledgeable yet Unobtrusive, Professional, Attractive, and Complimentary yet Not Hitting on You or Your Date, Quick-Witted, Sure-Footed, Never See an Empty Water Glass Service." This is a tall order, and many discriminating diners will penalize a waiter for things out of his or her control. The timing of the food service, for instance. It's not always the server's fault if the food does not come within your preferred hunger window. There are numerous variables at work to cause delays—a shiftless management, a hung-over line cook, a scallop vendor that didn't show. And none of them are your waiter's fault. Keep in mind also that you are also a part of the inevitable trickle-down economics of a restaurant— your lousy tip affects the busboy making seven dollars an hour, the sommelier, the breadbasket refill guy, and basically anyone who approaches your table. So keep all of them into account when you calculate your gratuity. And here's the feel-good part: when someone does give you good service, worthy of an over-tip, your hearty percentage will surely make their day (and possibly their rent payment) and make you feel like a benefactor or celebrity. Bonus: you'll get great service when you go back.

Lie When Necessary (free!)

It's fantastic when friends follow their dreams and throw themselves into creative pursuits. Your role is to support them and offer implausible solutions to their problems. But there comes a time, a day of reckoning as it were, when you are asked to witness the final product, and must not only sit through a three-hour documentary about cleft palate surgery in India, but also stick around for a focus group. If at any point in life, you are asked to share your "feedback" with a film's creators as they stand poised on a platform, daring you to be honest, *do not fall into their trap*. They may say, "Be totally, brutally honest," or, "We want your gut reaction," but they don't really mean it. If you venture forth with a criticism of any magnitude ("Did you really need that twenty-minute segment with the group hug?"), prepare for your friendship to pay the price. It's sort of like giving a close friend a negative assessment of a significant other: they will never get over it, and will harbor a simmering resentment toward you as long as they're involved with that relationship. So, in the spirit of selfless encouragement and positive reinforcement, why not give the panel compliments? Rack your brain for moving passages and original camerawork. If you can't think of any specifics, use vague terms like "tone" and "texture." Your friend will no doubt nod maniacally until you are done, and then you can sit back down and listen to everyone else deliver their damning criticisms, knowing that you may not have furthered the arts but that you have salvaged a friendship.

HUG IT OUT (FREE!)

 Everyone loves a hug. On the next slow, gray Tuesday morning, announce that you are giving out free hugs all day to any and all interested parties. An even better idea is to tell everyone that your coworker is giving out free hugs. They will love you for this.

BE A CRAPPY BAR BAND'S BIGGEST FAN ($–$$)

 Sometimes you just wanna rock, but the thought of shelling out seventy-five bucks to see Nickleback at the Globocon Arena just isn't in the cards. Instead, head out to smaller, independent, salty rock clubs that host unexpected, undiscovered, and under-hyped music scenes and you can see a rockin' show for ridiculously low ticket costs (seven dollars and two drink tickets, anyone?). Some of these shows might be god-awful, but any live music, played loud enough and accompanied by well whiskey and coke, is better than listening to some drunk twenty-three-year-old girl request Britney's "Womanizer" on the Internet jukebox for the fourth time. Most of the bands you will see in these establishments will never be heard from again, but there's always the chance you somehow stumble upon the next Nirvana, earning a lifetime's worth of "I saw them when" rock-snob gloating. And you can really make your night both memorable and charitable by rocking out in the front row, screaming for encores, buying the merchandise, and introducing yourself to other patrons as "Johnny DragonLayrs" biggest fans. You will make the band's night.

BRING BROWNIES TO THE
FIRE STATION ($)

 It never hurts to be on the good side of your local firemen. Let's face it, in a cynical and snark-filled world, the fireman represents the best that humankind has to offer. Why not whip up a bunch of brownies and take them down to Company 9 just to say, "Thanks for risking your life so idiots like me who leave a scented candle burning overnight can have a second chance"? Ideally the brownies should be homemade from scratch but straight-out-the-box is OK, too, as long as they look homemade. Just be sure to undercook them slightly—nobody likes a brittle brownie. You might decide to drop them off on a significant day (say,

September 11) or it could just be a spur-of-the-moment decision, a sincere gesture of your appreciation and thanks in ways that mere tax dollars can never express.

GIVE A STRANGER A COMPLIMENT (FREE!)

Compliments are easy to devise, but it's the delivery that many people stumble on. You don't want to sound overly solicitous, secretly bitchy, or sleazy/lurky. That's why women need to work on friendly, straightforward same-sex compliments and men should learn to compliment the ladies without an implied wolf-whistle. Here are some handy pointers:

Women

Turn Jealousy into Philanthropy! The next time you're out and about and you see a girl with a slammin' dress, to-die-for bag or just really, really cute shoes, instead of giving her a bitchy look and brushing by, stop for a minute and say, "I love your (dress/bag/shoes)." Do not then follow up with potentially undermining investigative questions like, "Where did you get it? Is it real? Is that last season?" Just let the friendly, selfless, no-strings-attached comment stand.

Men

Know the Line between Flattery and Harassment! It's what you say, and how you say it. Think *straightforward subtlety*. "That's a nice hat," could have numerous amorous overtones, all dependent on the delivery. If it's playful, flirty with a sly smile, the girl can interpret the compliment on her own. "That's a nice ass," however, is all straightforward, no subtlety, and is almost guaranteed to backfire with either a disgusted look or a slap—and not the good kind.

Everyone

Compliment an Old Person! Old people are grimly accustomed to being marginalized by a society that upholds Vanessa Hudgens as a cultural icon. They are used to being invisible. So, the next time you see someone in their AARP-brochure-receiving years, think of something frank and positive to say about their appearance, outfit, smile, attitude, etc., and just say it! You will be more beloved than their grandkids.

Compliment a Coworker! You likely spend more time with your coworkers than with family or friends. As such, you may grow to resent them. But try to see your coworkers in a different light, past their office personas. It's not just "Lecherous Ed from Sales" or "Harried Caroline from HR"—they are people, just like you. Think of a genuine and sincere compliment about their appearance, performance, or desktop wallpaper and say it loud enough so others can hear what a kind and thoughtful person you are.

Compliment a Fast Food Cashier! Behind every crisp french fry and frosty chocolate shake there is a real person, one with hopes and dreams, who must don a silly hat and a management-enforced smile. Instead of treating your local Burger King cashier like a vending machine, take a moment to express admiration for their hairstyle, lilting voice (if it's a drive-thru), or deft punching of cheeseburger-embossed cashier buttons. You'll help break up the monotony and brighten their day—and potentially score free dipping sauces!

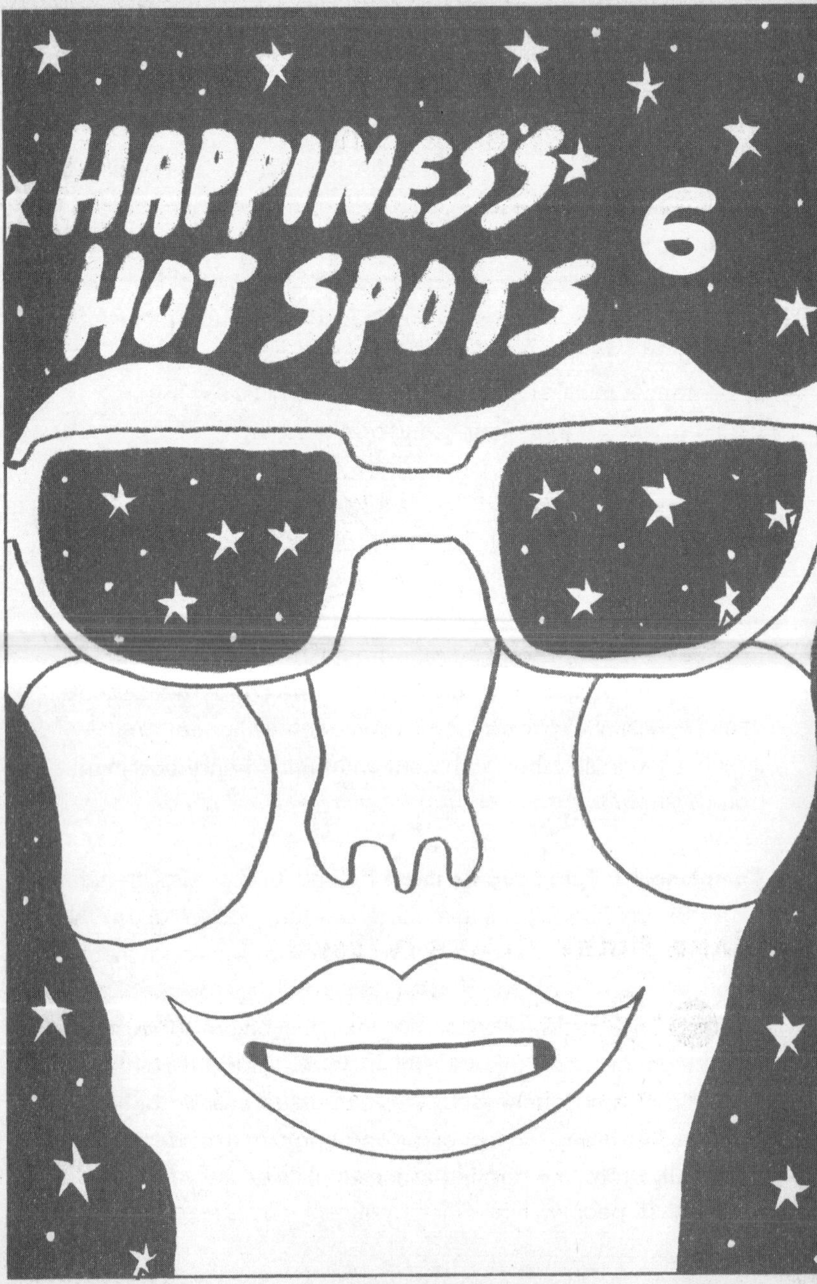
HAPPINESS HOT SPOTS
6

Destinations, venues, and states of mind

> "Remember that happiness is a way of travel—not a destination."
>
> —ROY M. GOODMAN

We're all born with a little bit of wanderlust. And for good reason—travel broadens the mind, exposes you to new ideas, architecture, and lifestyles, and is a fundamental source of happiness, even if the trip is just back to bed for a nap.

FAKE FIRST CLASS ($–$$)

 Why is it that even the most minor differences—free soft drinks, a red mat in front of the customer service representative, orchids in a waiting area, good coffee—can make life so much more enjoyable? The answer may lie in every person's secret belief that he or she is better than other people. First-class treatment encourages this

delusion. But as we all know, this most rarefied method of comportment is also the antithesis of affordable. A random spot check of a first-class ticket from New York to Los Angeles reveals a price tag of $2,883.50. One way. What's a budget happiness hunter to do? Fake first class! While you can't do much about the grim physical environment, lack of leg room, or irritating fellow passengers, there are things you can do to make seat 54F feel more like seat 2A. With a little know-how and planning, you can bring on board all you'll need for a populist interpretation of first-class dinner service. It's all about preparation:

Three Ounces to Happiness Most airlines still have restrictions on liquids, so bringing a bottle of Bordeaux is out. However, have you ever noticed what else comes in tiny bottles? That's right—booze! Stop at your neighborhood liquor mart and pick up a handful of tiny vodkas, rums, or scotches, and stick those in your plastic baggie in lieu of shampoo . . . there's likely some at the hotel, anyway. There's not much you can do about mixers, but most flight attendants are actually pretty cool about bringing you a small can of tonic water between the scheduled beverage services.

Create the Mood Another important means of preparation is a hot lemony towel. Before you depart for the airport, simply squeeze a lemon on a moist washcloth, then stop by the restroom en route to your gate, douse in hot water, wring out, and place in a Ziploc bag. This might seem like a lot of extra work but it actually helps break up the mind-numbing monotony of the modern travel experience and gives you a refreshing spa-in-the-sky experience midway through the flight. Make a habit of offering the hot towel to yourself and either stating aloud or thinking: "Don't mind if I do!"

Be Your Own Gourmet Chef Most commercial flights charge eight dollars for a hard ham sandwich and small tin of Pringles. Fight the system! Prepare a meal and a series of snacks ahead of time. And think swanky: no handful of trail mix or Terminal 3 turkey wrap is going to elevate your experience. Finger sandwiches are remarkably easy to make, convenient to snack on, and can come in a delightful array of varieties based on what's in your fridge postdeparture. Cucumber and jalapeño cream cheese. Turkey, cheddar, and avocado. Peanut butter and jelly. Simply make a sandwich, divide into fours, cut off the crusts, and you'll be ready for high tea in high altitudes.

Finally, happy seatmates equals happy traveling. If you're able to bring enough supplies to give the first-class treatment to your entire row, you'll be an in-flight hero and amass precious travel karma for years to come.

HELSINKI? HELL, YES! ($$–$$$)

Large public squares, chummy locals, harborside dining, fab modern architecture, and attractive blondes—Helsinki may just be happiness heaven. Stay in a swishy hotel with the very best in Nordic modernist decor for $110 a night (Klaus K). Frequent Hietsu Beach, replete with beautiful people and minimal bikinis. Hit up the Arctic Icebar (located inside the nightclub UNIQ) where a nominal admission fee (about twelve dollars) buys you a second layer of warm clothing (this icy bar is kept at 23 degrees Fahrenheit) and a complimentary shot of Finlandia vodka. Visit a Finnish sauna—there are about two million, so you won't have to look far. Most will cost you between five and eight dollars. Bring a towel into the sauna if you must, but you really should go native and go naked—this can be a liberating experience.

HAPPINESS HINT

Sunglasses at Night: Pro or Con?

Pro: If you're traveling, it's time to abandon old attitudes and embrace new styles. Why not wear sunglasses at night? You're on vacation!

Con: Yes, but do you want your vacation photos to say, "I'm a tool, and I don't care who knows it"? This style is about as acceptable as fanning a handful of hundred dollar bills in front of you.

Pro: But if you're in an Arctic Circle–proximate location, the sun is actually out! Sunglasses at night are purely functional, not pretentious.

Con: The sun might still be out later than usual in certain parts of the Northern or Southern hemispheres, but it's certainly not strong enough to require a pair of shades.

Pro: I just want to stand out and possibly get laid. Doesn't an accessory like sunglasses at night help attract attention?

Con: Maybe. But they might also be a Scandinavian dealbreaker. If you must don a kicky nightlife accessory, try a fedora. Save the shades for your morning-after brunch.

Nouveau North Dakota ($$)

 When most people plan a holiday, they look for excitement. But how about traveling to a town where you, the traveler, *are* the excitement? Which brings us to the less splashy states, sprinkled across the Pacific Northwest, Midwest, and Southeast, destinations that don't necessarily have sexy big cities or recognizable local cuisine but that are nonetheless worth your precious travel dime. Take North Dakota, one of America's least populous states with only 635,867 residents. An unprecedented oil boom and strong year for farming have left the state relatively flush. This means a happy, secure citizenry not in the death throes brought on by McMansion foreclosures and job loss—talk about a tourist attraction! Plus you'll find mountain beauty, charming historic districts, hiking, snowmobiling, and hunting galore for those tired of a cosseted, fey urban lifestyle. Other seemingly under-the-radar states worth exploring such as Iowa, Minnesota, and Rhode Island will no doubt welcome you and introduce you to local customs, legal or not.

Buy Local ($$–$$$)

 According to *Travel & Leisure* magazine, people are traveling within the United States more and more. It's affordable, it involves less time in the air and more on the ground, and there are fifty states to explore. Here are some of the best (and worst) domestic cities to visit based on a 2008 nationwide survey (*Travel & Leisure*, October 2008):

Best Places for Peace and Quiet

Santa Fe What could be more peaceful than a violet butte, an alabaster dessert, coyotes braying in the distance? Santa Fe's all-encompassing natural beauty and resistance to large-scale development make it the perfect place to relax and tune out. Also: delicious Tex-Mex cuisine.

Charleston The South is good for relaxin', that's for sure. Perhaps it's the abundance of porches, the heat, the wisteria, or the endless glasses of sweet tea and/or bourbon. But the friendly, warm, welcoming people are what really shocks the system into a state of relaxed contentment. Y'all come back now, y'hear!

Honolulu While not the most budget-friendly destination due to the staggering cost of air travel, if you've racked up enough miles to get you there, you'll find many soul-soothing options for the happily frugal. The most obvious, of course, are the beaches—all public land, all gorgeous. Hawaii also has solid public transportation (the bus is $2), free nightly hula and fire-dancing shows, excellent street food, endless hiking opportunities, and the notoriously laid-back mahalo culture. Finally, what could be more soothing and peaceful than our new Hawaiian-born president?

(Worst Place for Peace and Quiet: **New York.** "The city that never sleeps" is a sometimes painfully apt title.)

Most Attractive Populace

Miami Bienvenido a Miami! Cultural diversity meets a party-all-night ethos—with a tan. While the flashy dressing and often mind-numbing salsa music can sometimes make you feel like you're in an echo chamber of bad prints and bass-heavy beats, it is the best place in the United States for unabashed eye candy.

San Diego You stay classy! Despite the proximity to Shamu and killer burritos, San Diego is chock full of hotties. From the rowdy and collegiate blue lamp district to salty downtown dives and hidden romantic Pacific Beach restaurants, everywhere you turn you'll find an attractive stranger.

Austin Mmm, they make 'em cute in Texas. Calculate big sky country wholesome good looks with Austin's alt-rock and mumble-core film industry and you have an artful blend of cowboy and creative-industry hotness.

(Least Attractive Populace: **Philadelphia**? Outrageous. Gino's Cheesesteaks rule!)

Best Food and Dining
New Orleans The culinary fireworks of Cajun and Creole dining and the unwaveringly odd and endearing spirit of the city make New Orleans an ideal food destination. Po-boys, pralines, gumbo, catfish: just go easy on the hurricanes.

New York You've got your Bouley, your Batali, your Meyer, your Morimoto. And even dreamy Tom Collichio is back at an actual stove. Yes, you'll pay an arm and a leg, but there's also $2 bagels and $3 pizza slices, so perhaps it evens out.

San Francisco The city by the bay has a rich culinary history, and is so rabidly locovore that you'll know, down to the row, where your fresh summer corn salad came from. Best bets: The Slanted Door, Zuni, Quince. Or visit the Ferry Building Farmer's Market on any given Saturday for a total immersion in Bay Area food fetishism.

(Worst Food and Dining: **Atlanta**. Apparently *Travel & Leisure* readers haven't come around to "haute grits.")

REDISCOVER COLLEGE BARS ($)

 Ah, college. Those halcyon days when a "tough schedule" meant classes started at 10 a.m., when you were always broke but somehow always had beer, and when "partying" was not just an activity but an all-encompassing state of mind. Relive the glory days at one of your town's college pubs. Enjoy the watered-down well drinks and nightly specials (Two-For Tuesday, Thirsty Thursdays) and rediscover the afford-able, filling college diet of 2 a.m. pizza slices or Taco Bell. Sway along to the current hot hits ("Who is this Akon?" you might ask.) and listen to the drinking songs, all while reminiscing about your alma mater and trying not to look like the lurky old person at the college bar. To this end: although flirting with college students is a fun and harmless vocation, actually going back to their fraternity/sorority/dorm room is not recommended under any circumstances.

SWIMMIN' HOLES (FREE!)

 Whoever coined the term, "The best things in life are free," was likely lazin' by a swimmin' hole in the summertime. Most swimmin' holes are by their very nature difficult to find, involving backcountry roads and a close, personal relationship with a local tackle shop owner. Be prepared to swap tall tales in order to be given access to the right route. But once you get there, all you need is a picnic blanket, towels, some trunks, and an obligation-free afternoon, and happiness is guaranteed.

STRETCH THE DOLLAR ($–$$$)

Why not go where the dollar is still worth something? Make your next vacation destination a place where American currency is celebrated and embraced. The more remote, unusual, or unexpected the better, because nothing ruins a good vacation more than proximity to other vacationing Americans.

Tierra del Fuego, Argentina It's the end of the world. Literally. Travel to this southernmost spot, where, due to the fall of the Argentine peso in 2001, swanky spas and hearty slabs of beef are well under market rate. The whole island is a Tax Free Zone, two- to three-star hotels start at $60 and a five-star spa hotel can be had for $300 a night (Los Cauquenes Resort & Spa).

Saigon, Vietnam Sure, you've heard about it. But perhaps it's time to actually take a trip, and not in the Apocalypse Now, psychedelic freak-out sense. Vietnam is not merely home to horrific war atrocities; it also has pristine sandy beaches and delicious French-inspired cuisine, and the dollar is holding strong against the Vietnamese dong. For instance: a king room at the five-star Park Hyatt Saigon is just $230 a night (the same would set you back about $500 stateside).

Krakow, Poland Prague is so premillennial. See what's crackin' in Krakow, the latest post-Communist country deemed cool by the *Blackbook* set. Dine like a king on pierogis (for pennies!) on Szeroka Street, then hit the clubs in the Kazimierz district—such as the red-hot Goraczka, whose online literature promises "great atmosphere, positive freaked people, outstanding guests, and best black'n'dance music." Simmer down at night's end with a little jazz and wartime Parisian décor in the Stalowe Magnolie bar, famous for hosting jazz greats both celebrated and obscure—after a few dozen vodkas, who can really tell the difference?

Puerto Morelos, Mexico While much of the once-pristine Mexican coastal land has been swiftly transformed into all-inclusive megaresorts, Puerto Morelos remains a staunchly sleepy fishing village on the Yucatán coast (known, in marketing terms, as the Mayan Riviera). Sit in outdoor restaurants and dine on cheap nopales rellenos (stuffed cactus) and margaritas, kick it on the zocolo (a shady public square), enjoy beachside cervezas at Sarah's Place, a locally beloved beach café/shack and, later, dine some of the finest seafood on the Caribbean (at thirteen pesos to the dollar, no less). And, with no beer-bonging spring breakers or Prada-clad luxury vacationers to implicate you as awful-by-association, you can easily attain the approval of affable locals.

MUSEUMS OF QUESTIONABLE CULTURAL VALUE ($)

Every time you visit a new city, there's overwhelming pressure to go to a museum. Society tells us that we are essentially uncouth Mountain–Dew–swilling slobs if we don't manage to make time in the itinerary for Flemish still lifes and crumbly Grecian urns. But does anyone really, truly enjoy trudging those hushed, gilded halls? On your next jaunt, how about checking out museums that curate a different set of values? They call it "popular culture" for a reason:

Burt Reynolds Museum Jupiter, Florida ($5 entrance fee)

Where else can you behold the *Deliverance* canoe, the boots worn in *The Best Little Whorehouse in Texas*, the original 1977 Pontiac Trans Am Firebird driven in *Smokey and the Bandit*, and signed head shots from every long-tressed '70s megababe imaginable (Cher! Crystal Gale!)? The Burt Reynolds Museum has it all, plus a gift shop where you can procure a charcoal sketch of a shirtless (but cowboy hat–clad) Burt or an official Burt Reynolds coffee mug, which ensures that you will never endure another awkward silence at the coffee machine again.

Liberace Museum Las Vegas, Nevada ($10 entrance fee)

All of the self-styled "playas" out there rocking their CZ bling need to visit the glittering shrine to the man who started it all. Who else could be so bold to commission a rhinestone-encrusted grand piano? See for yourself Liberace's piano-shaped ring, adorned with 260 individual diamonds. Or the Rolls Royce clad in mirrored tiles, etched with a bracing galloping horse motif. There's even a re-created master bedroom from Liberace's Palm Springs estate, replete with a Louis XV desk and enough velvet and Moser crystal to stun even the most austere modern minimalist into reverential silence.

Museum of Quackery St. Paul, Minnesota ($11 entrance fee)

Explore the history of medical quackery inside the Science Museum of Minnesota. Your inner hedonist will marvel at the history of patent medicines (many quack doctors used cocaine, morphine, and alcohol as ingredients in their "cure-alls"), and you can view antique medical instruments, eyeball massagers, creepy vibrating chairs (supposedly to cure intestinal distress) and a "Foot-Operated Breast Enlarger," which, although it was completely ineffectual, had brisk sales up to the mid-1970s.

YOUR BED (FREE–$$$$)

 Sometimes you'll find the greatest journey is to sweet unconsciousness. Make your bed as cozy and luxurious as possible, and you'll feel like every night is a trip to an exotic land of vibrant color and silken textures. Here's what you'll need to reach this most desirable destination:

Sensible Splurge—A Featherbed You spend a third of your life in bed, so why not make it the cushiest experience possible? Splurging on a nice featherbed ($99–$200) can bring you years of sound sleep and cozy euphoria. Your former "place to crash" will now become a Fluffy Cloud of Dreams, where all of life's worries melt away.

The Perfect Pillow If your pillows have been around since the Reagan administration, it's time for an upgrade. Back and stomach sleepers need thinner pillows, so the head is not thrown too far forward, while side sleepers need a fluffier, thicker pillow to fill in the gap between the head and the shoulders. You don't need to blow the bank: a simple, regular-size feather pillow is just as effective as space-age synthetics and can be found in the $20–$40 range.

Heavenly Bedding Pick a cool-toned color palette for your duvet cover and sheets: palace blue, deep citrus, lavender, slate gray, and dusky rose all encourage lounging and dreaming. Choose a higher thread count (at least 600) and high-quality cotton. It's better to have nicer sheets that last longer than a rotating carousel of coarse budget sheets.

Stuffed Animals If you are single, and still sleep with a stuffed animal or two, that is absolutely fine—let 'em join the party. But just make sure to discreetly store Fluffles under the bed if company comes over.

Bedside Accessories Fill a large carafe with lemon water for easy-access refreshment throughout the night. Fresh flowers are also a nice touch. Nature CDs (crickets, whale sounds) should be cleared with your partner before utilizing.

Nap Time Even without these plush extras, sometimes a good nap is all you need to improve your day. The couch is the uncontested king of all naps. Have a throw blanket handy, get in a comfy position and let drowsiness descend. If you find yourself at work in dire need of a nap, there is no shame in constructing a "nap space" under your desk with pillow, comforter, and cashmere eye mask. Just remember to lock your office door, or, if you are in a cube or open office space, construct a curtain that hangs down over your desk so you may doze unnoticed.

7
Shameless
CONSUMERISM

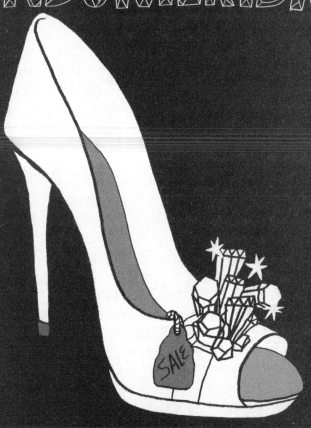

You are what you buy.
Shouldn't it be really pretty?

"Whoever said money can't buy happiness didn't know where to shop."

—GERTRUDE STEIN

It might be true that we all have too much "stuff." But remember that consumerism in moderation can be quite healthy! Learn to harness the shopper's high—without necessarily spending a single dime.

THE TAO OF THE ETERNAL SHOPPER ($–$$$$)

For some people, shopping is a game—one with no rules, fierce competition, bad Muzak, and no clear winners. But it doesn't have to be. Here's a secret from people who shop: shopping with a specific purpose, whether for an event, last-minute gift, or pointed, specific, time-sensitive purpose, is a baffling, awful ordeal. Even if you love shopping. Ditto for "shopping on the cheap," looking relentlessly for sales and bargains, forgoing random, creative impulse buys for sensible shopping excursions (e.g., the twice-annual "trip to the outlet mall!"). On the contrary, you should consider yourself *always* shopping, that is, always on the lookout for a good deal, a true must-have, a rare gem, a perfect gift, a flattering party outfit. "Shop" all the time, and if and when you find something truly worthy of your consumer dollar, you'll just know it. It could be in an airport lounge in Auckland or a bargain bin in Bhutan, just keep an open mind wherever you go, trust your retail intuition, purchase when you really, truly want to, not when you have to, and then squirrel away that item for the rainy day, wedding, birthday, or job interview. Think of the delicious feeling that comes with already having a host gift or something to wear for the last-minute event. You'll be gently rejecting soulless consumption, avoiding harried "doorbuster" sales that demean everyone involved, and, best of all, never have to "go shopping" again!

COUTURE WINDOW SHOPPING! (FREE!)

  When it comes to high-class window shopping, stick to the upper echelon: designer boutiques. Prada's flagship in Milan, Christian Dior in Paris, and Bergdorf Goodman in New York are assured to bring you happiness, even if you're just browsing— *especially* if you're just browsing. And if you happen to be a guy who's been dragged along on a shopping expedition, take heart in the fact that many high-end boutiques have a comfortable couch that you may sit on (really upper-tier places might offer you espresso or champagne). Besides getting to see your significant other in smokin' new ensembles, you also get to view girls who aren't your girlfriend in various states of undress. (Note: do not point this out to your girlfriend.)

How to Get Fantastic Service without Spending One Thin Dime

A few key accessories, a nice British upper-crust accent, and some hints from the pros and you'll have snotty salesladies eating out of your begloved palm.

Confidential to the Ladies Search through your closet for the one really high-end shopping bag that you have furtively saved. Wrap a sweater in tissue (carefully) and sling this around your shoulder—salespeople always pay more attention if it looks as if you're on a retail tear. Wear a piece of statement jewelry on your wedding finger. The bigger and gaudier the bling (faux or not) the better, as the idea of a bored gold-digging wife is infinitely appealing to a commission-hungry salesperson. Bring a digital camera, and do a makeshift photo shoot in the dressing room. Say, "I'm just sending these to Nigel." "Nigel" is code for your personal shopper, and every salesperson knows it. Ask demanding questions such as, "Is this *highland* Alpaca?" or "Do you overnight to Dubai?" Pick really hideous, over-the-top pieces, like animal print Versace, and force the obsequious salesperson to muster up a compliment.

Confidential to the Gents Wear sunglasses inside. Refer often to your BlackBerry. Say you don't have much time. It doesn't really matter, a single male in a couture shop is like a fist-sized gold nugget in a stream of silty flakes—you are a treasure. They know you're probably (1) shopping for a girlfriend/wife and (2) clueless and afraid. As such they will flatter and flirt until you've made that two-thousand-dollar purchase that your wife or girlfriend will be thrilled and mildly confused by. Since men rarely, if ever, put things on hold, if you wish to soak up the (usually quite attractive) salesgirl attention and feel like a big shot, you can always purchase something extravagant and then discreetly return the item at a later date.

Important Note This activity is only free if you don't buy anything that you can't return. Beware of the impulse sale buy—if you feel one coming on, fake an emergency at your summer chateau and make your escape. Put an item on hold for authenticity.

BUY A BIKE! ($$)

Gas is expensive, public transportation is slow and pungent. Walking can get boring, and you're not together enough to pull off a Zip Car or rideshare commitment. The answer to this transportation quagmire? A shiny new bike! Well, "shiny" is relative. So is "new." Unless you are a mountain bike/Performance Gear–type person, a good used bike can be your affordable and oh-so-chic new way to get from point A to point B. Look for Schwinn or Raleigh models from the '60s or '70s. Your local used bike emporium (or eBay or Craigslist) no doubt has tons of fly bikes that are looking for a new home, priced in the $50–$200 range. Some cities even have police bike sales, where unclaimed bikes go from $10–$15, plus an intrinsic sense of toughness that comes from riding a felon's bike. Once you select your new bike, you can trick it out with a basket and bell. Go easy on other accessories like wheel ribbons or mini customized license plate, lest you look like a creepy man-child or girly woman. Beyond its stylish lines and eco-friendly cache, riding a bike gives you a sense of determination over your world—you can glide through traffic, go the wrong way down one-way streets, and park wherever you damn well please. And there's just no end to the attractiveness factor of a girl, in a skirt, on a bike, although be warned that the skirt should not be short enough to literally stop traffic.

STRATEGIC SAMPLING (FREE!)

There are so many ways to get free stuff while shopping. "Samples" are tiny, adorably packaged vehicles for retail employees to entice you into buying their wares, and are usually found in the cosmetic and perfume counters. Great for travel or for a weeklong game of fragrance roulette, you can amass handfuls of the very latest, most expensive perfume and cologne samples just by politely requesting them. Now, you might feel like this is taking advantage of the poor, scrapping, multibillion-dollar luxury brand conglomerates, but take heart—the markup on perfume is absurdly high. Just approach the counter of your choice and say, "I'm looking to buy a gift for my [girlfriend/boyfriend/wealthy in-law's] birthday, but I don't know what they like. Could I get a few samples of the latest fragrances to bring home to [him/her]?" And open your palms. The same is true of many high-end cosmetic counters. Sometimes they can be stingy, or won't give up the samples until after you've made a colossal purchase, but in these troubled times even the whiff of a retail decision on your part will be met with joy and enthusiasm. "It never hurts to ask" should be your mantra, and ask you should, for lip gloss samples, eye cream samples, tiny mascara samples, and anything else you see. Again, framing your request for "the very latest" puts you in the category of cutting-edge tastemaker, someone who is an influencer, someone who should be wooed and courted in order to become a brand ambassador for Stila Cherry Crush Lip Stain or NARS Showgirl Eyeliner.

TEST-DRIVE YOUR DREAM CAR (FREE!)

 So we all (vaguely) remember the scene in *Scent of a Woman* where a blind Al Pacino and cute lil' Chris O'Donnell test-drive a Ferarri through the streets of Manhattan. Hoo-ahh! You can get the same thrill, without the overacting. Unlike in the movies, where a blind man and a seventeen-year-old prep student can roll out of a Manhattan car dealership in a Ferrari 348, most high-end European car manufacturers require a valid driver's license and the gift of sight. Some will actually extend "incentives" (Bose headphones, hundred-dollar AmEx gift certificates) to entice you to test-drive their luxury rides. But you'll likely only get one of these plum offers if you reside in certain high-income zip codes, use a platinum credit card with a $300,000 limit, or are the current owner of a luxury vehicle. But the drive, not the freebie, is the goal here. Most upscale cars (Bentley, Maserati, Aston-Martin, Mercedes) have similarly upscale websites. Simply go to one and use the zip code locator to find a dealer in your area, place a phone call, say you would like to test drive a car, and schedule an appointment. It's just that easy.

> ### HAPPINESS HINT
>
> Have a specific make and model in mind when you call. You want to appear serious, educated, and ready to sign on the dotted line, so if you call a Bentley dealer and say you'd like to test drive, "um, a black one?" you might not get the most accommodating reaction.

In most cases, the car salesman (or Customer Service Liason) will roll with you, but no worries! Just say you want to test out the sound system and tune him or her out. Butter him or her up and see if you can take the car off-road. Be sure to embellish your net worth a bit with offhand references to wintering in Gstaad or hitching a ride on "Ron Air" (Ron Burkle's private jet).

A terrific way of getting out of the uncomfortable financing talk in some pleasingly minimalist back office is to set your cell phone alarm and then say, in a pained expression, that your wife or sister has just gone into labor . . . but you'll be in touch! Then give the salesman a fake phone number and be on your merry way.

Sparkle, Shoes, and Shades ($–$$$)

Fashion is a fickle beast, and an awfully tough one to chase. In this regard, men's and women's fashion magazines are right: accessories are everything. The upside of this truism is that it's a hell of a lot easier (and less expensive) to overhaul your look each season by making minor adjustments than it is to chuck a closetful of origami-inspired austerity for this season's embellished boho. Brush off your basics and invest in a few new accessories to make them look—and feel—fresh and updated. See what's on the runways, knowing that the fashion trickle-down is swift, and choose the most reasonable facsimiles of your favorite looks. Also note: finding something in your favorite store then scouting around online for a cheaper price will maximize savings, limit risk, and give you a fun new way to procrastinate at work.

Sparkle For women, if cocktail rings make another comeback, you're in luck—giant fake gems are relatively easy to come by and give you that sophisticate sparkle in one wallet-friendly swoop. So is faux-gold and pretty much anything related to the "tribal" trend. For men, belts and cufflinks are basically the only ways to easily update your wardrobe, but this isn't to say they don't make a significant impression. An awesome pair of McQueen-inspired skull cufflinks or a minimalist Philip Lim belt can take you from clueless drone to suave and in-the-know. It's quite easy to readjust your wardrobe with these quick fixes, while saving the splurge for an investment piece that transcends flash-in-the-pan trends, something timeless and elegant—a fantastic watch, for instance.

Shoes Knockoffs don't work on your feet. Shoes should always be well-constructed and made of quality materials (they take quite a beating, after all), and are worth shelling out a bit more for. And on a sheer stylistic level, it's better to sport a tasteful homage to Balenciaga's eight-hundred-dollar stacked heel than a witless Payless copy. It's been said before, and it should be said again: a really killer pair of heels can transform a women's whole outlook on life, so don't be afraid to purchase a truly thrilling pair once (or twice) a year. Men, you have no idea how much your shoes say about you. Bad buckled shoes equal aging frat boy, imitation-croc loafers mean troubling Euro-trash, but bespoke leather shoes, classic cowboy boots, or just a really good basic sneaker impart "worldly but unpretentious," "basic but not boring," and "comfortable but not deadbeat."

Shades A fabulous pair of sunglasses can radically change your look, but here's a word to the wise: never buy them online. The odds of actually selecting a pair of sunglasses that look good on you without trying them on are frightfully slim. Pop into your local sunglasses shop and try on as many as you like. A classic aviator looks good on most people, as does, for a woman, glamorous Jackie O–style oversize lenses. Experiment with new

materials and current silhouettes that are outside your comfort zone, and once you make your purchase, wear them at all times (except at night). They will bring last year's wardrobe right up to date, and you'll look intriguingly incognito.

GIVE THE GIFT OF SOMEONE ELSE'S LOVE ($–$$)

If you are crafty, the obvious choice when giving a gift is to DIY. If you panic at the sight of rubber cement and knitting needles, don't sweat it! You can *buy* handmade gifts, thereby supporting someone who's trying to make their way in the world by using their God-given talents. Furthermore, your money will be going directly to a person instead of a faceless corporation or soul-crushing chain of middlemen. Visit sites like Etsy.com or GetCrafty.com—it's just as easy as ordering from a big box store, and you usually get a handwritten note along with your purchase. No, it wasn't technically your hands that made the macramé beer cozy or rain slicker out of bubble wrap, but you can bask in the glow of second-hand creativity.

GIVE YOUR ELECTRONICS A NEW LOOK ($$)

People who customize their iPods with crystal beads and outfit their laptops with nineteenth-century typewriter keyboards are lame, right? Or are they on to something? If you can't muster up the funds for a shiny new piece of technology right now, why not take what you already have and give it a makeover? After all, you spend most of your waking hours with your computer or iPhone—doesn't it

deserve a little flair? There are all kinds of independent crafts-people that can turn everything from a BlackBerry to a clunky Dell desktop into couture creations. You can adorn your laptop with flames, howling wolves, or other makeout-van staples, or take the classier route and purchase a plastic casing for your iPhone that has your name embossed in elegant letterpress. Buy a saucy wristlet-purse for your iPod for stylish portability, or enlist the help of a Velcro expert to discreetly attach it to your favorite coat. If you're the type of person who thinks that a small dog in an argyle sweater is adorable, you can even purchase a hoodie for your electronic device, complete with pouch for headphones.

THE ONE-SPLURGE-A-YEAR PLAN ($$$$+)

We're only human, and sometimes we become besotted with something that we just can't live without. It can be as simple as a new toaster oven or something radical like a yacht or second home. On the one-splurge-a-year plan, you can allot a portion of your income to this one exciting purchase, and ensure that it's top-notch. Rather than blowing your money on hundreds of tiny, useless, nearly disposable consumer items to curb your appetite for consumption, focus on this one thing—designer handbag, motorcycle, leather jacket, professional-level camera, new computer, or espresso machine— and hold off on any frivolous spending until you've accrued enough funds for this one very special splurge.

For Example: a Really, Really Good Hairdryer

If you scrimp on certain necessities, they'll come back to haunt you. You might regard the humble hairdryer as a mere blip on

your yearly consumer radar, but a high-quality ceramic ionic hairdryer will improve your life in ways you can't possibly imagine. The science behind it is a complex and closely guarded secret. Frederick Fekkai may have the blueprints for the first model in a vault somewhere in Zurich. But whatever innovations are responsible for the frizz-defying powers, the results are fantastic: static-free and quick drying, it runs whisper-quiet, and looks and feels luxurious and infinitely svelte. Obliterating bad hair days, and all but negating the purchase of overly expensive shampoos, you can even "cut back" on your every-six-week haircuts, so smooth and healthy will your hair look. And think about it: isn't great hair better than some dumb Coach bag that will be out of style in four months? Yes. No matter how much ramen you have to eat, this is an important one.

risky business

8

Enjoy the thrill of ditching your comfort zone

> *"Happiness is nothing more than good health and a bad memory."*
>
> —ALBERT SCHWEITZER

What is life without a little risk? Learn to face your fears, trample your trepidation, and live on the edge—without going over it.

ONE, TWO, THREE—BACKYARD BUNGEE! (FREE–$)

Yes, this was a '90s trend popularized by the quasi-tragic Dan Corteze on *MTV Sports*. You also might associate bungee jumping with pasty tourists in Dingo T-shirts making their way up to a platform until a hale crew of hearty Aussies cajole them to take the plunge. This is all true. But it's also true that the thrill of the free fall is quite real, euphoric, and less time-consuming and claustrophobic than skydiving or Space Camp. That said, there are ways to experience this rush in your very own backyard! First, you'll need ten bungee cords. I'm sure there's a handful in your car's trunk, but if not, it's a perfectly good excuse to knock on your cute neighbor's door and ask to borrow a few. Connect five to seven of them together in one long rope. Then, use the remaining bungee cords to make a harness. The construction of the harness should maximize bounce and minimize crotch pain; always use an accent pillow as padding. Have a friend help you attach the rope to a tree branch or overhead beam using a standard Boy Scout sailor's knot. Finally, drag a mattress or trampoline outside in the very likely event that the bungee cords do not support your weight. (Also, be sure not to attempt from a high enough perch to cause injury.) Then, one, two, three—backyard bungee!

MIX '80S SITCOMS WITH LEGAL OPIATES (FREE–$)

 Abusing prescription medications is not advocated by the author by any means. At the same time, as long as you're down with a hacking chest cold, why not alternate swigs of the Magic Syrup with discovering how mind-blowingly racially insensitive those '80s sitcoms really were. *Perfect Strangers* is a good starting point, but steel yourself for *Diff'rent Strokes*. Top off your evening with season two of *Webster,* or the entire *Three's Company* oeuvre, and you'll wake up the next day glad to live in a world where broad, slapstick jokes at the expense of foreigners, black people, and gay men don't necessarily warrant a laugh track. You also may or may not have recovered from your cold. If not . . . repeat as necessary!

START YOUR OWN DATING SERVICE (FREE!)

 The trouble with dating websites is that the margin of error is so high. A date procured online is more likely to be unspeakably bad than even marginally good, and most resourceful singles tend to meet their special someone online only after committing to the volume theory. Dating experts say that most people meet their mates through friends of friends. Just think—you could be that "friend of a friend," that crucial cog in the social machine that brings Erin and Josh, Alicia and Dave, Steve and Jay together, forever! And you don't even need a fancy online platform, just a spiral-bound notebook and a thinking cap.

Place all the single guys you know in one column. Then all the single girls in another. Repeat for your gay friends. Then, using a pencil (you might need to erase and start over), begin lining up potential matches! Your pencil will serve as Cupid's arrow. The next step is arranging "the setup," where you must risk your own friendships and credibility to see if a love

HAPPINESS HINT

Many times you can spare yourself the e-cajoling and logistical problems of a setup by arranging for a "group setting" meet-up, a seemingly casual get-together with the singular goal of hooking up two of your friends. This has its pros (less pressure on the prospective couple, you get to actually witness the dynamic, live) and cons (you must be "on" all night—alert, discreet, and subtly encouraging). The worst case scenario: total misfire and public humiliation of one or both parties. The best case scenario? They just snuck off in a cab together!

match is made. This can be easily done via email: simply email the more adventurous half of the potential couple, saying there's someone you think they'd really like to meet. Test the waters and see how receptive they are. Then do the same with the other half of the setup, but this time say that a friend of yours is *dying* to meet them. (A little flattery never hurts.) Arrange a neutral, low-pressure date: after-work drinks or afternoon coffee. Then, call or email each to follow up! Encourage a second date if both parties seem intrigued but tentative, and if the date was an unmitigated disaster, quickly erase that particular connection and try again with someone else. This might sound like a lot of work, but the payoff is immense: imagine being toasted and feted at their wedding, having their child named after you, knowing their future happiness is all dependent on you, and, like the Italian code of *omerta*, you will never speak of this incident, but they will be indebted to you for life.

HOME-CURE YOUR HANGOVER ($)

 Everything in moderation. But if this truism slipped your mind last night somewhere around martini number two, take heart—there are many ways to help minimize this condition. While there is no known cure-all, you can take a few smart steps to assuage the physical (pounding headache, dry mouth) and metaphysical (Why did you tip that cute Aussie bartender $40 on a $60 tab? Why did you text your crush in the cab ride home? *Why* did you then get on effing Facebook and change your status to "Horny"?) pain, getting you closer to that mystical point in the day when you realize, like a phoenix rising miraculously from the ashes, that the hangover has lifted.

Stage One Hangover: Minimal
Diagnosis You're lucky. You either stayed with one beverage (white wine, vodka and soda) or drank in moderation, but for

whatever reason, you wake up feeling, while a little fuzzy and uncoordinated, at least remotely like yourself. Bravo, and consider patenting this unique combination of liquors.

Cure Have a just-in-case Advil, drink plenty of water, and keep your iTunes set to Air, Morcheeba, Enya, and other mid-1990s ambient music.

Stage Two Hangover: Moderate

Diagnosis "It's going to be OK." That's what you must tell yourself for the next eight to nine hours while you're stuck in your cubicle, reading the same report five times on a screen that seems to be vibrating, and reacting excessively frankly to coworkers' basic questions. For example, your manager says, "How's it going?" You respond, "I have the runs!"

Cure Start your day with a heroically grease-laden fast food breakfast sandwich: McDonald's McGriddle, Burger King Croissanwich, or Dunkin' Donuts Egg and Cheese Bagel. Lemonade can be a great hangover beverage, but a giant Coke will work as well. Pop an Alka-Seltzer or handful of Advil midday and swish some mouthwash to mask any post-booze whiff.

Stage Three Hangover: Severe

Diagnosis Things start out terrific. You dive into the shower, then arrive at work with a spring in your step and a list of brilliant mental notes. You are hilariously jazzed, focused, and ready to rock. You are also still drunk. The best thing to do is exploit these early hours of manic energy, when your body is still processing the toxic byproducts of all that bourbon and hasn't gotten around to that unpleasant part where said toxins trigger your stomach lining to void its contents.

Cure Cancel or make an excuse to get out of all meetings around 11 a.m., which is about the time when things go from "coming up roses" to "coming up . . ." well, you know. Try to take solace in the handicapped stall. Subsist the rest of the day on ginger ale and promises never to drink again.

Stage Four Hangover: Terminal

Diagnosis All you're likely able to handle is a wobbly trip to the bathroom and a glass of Crystal Light or Vitamin Water (for some reason, plain water is repulsive to the truly hungover.)

Cure Take one of your friend's painkillers that you "borrowed" after their minor foot operation and submit to a day of Bravo TV: *Top Design, Top Chef, Flipping Out*. What you need now is predictable reality competitions with a life-affirming slice of gay. The painkiller helps your headache and, more importantly, makes the demons go away—you know, those pesky fellows that dance

HAPPINESS HINT

Calling in sick is a huge source of happiness. Remember the four basic excuses for calling in sick when struck by a brutal hangover—the "FSCP" rule: Food Poisoning, Sinus Infection, Cable Guy Is Coming, and Personal Day. None of these are likely to be questioned, as long as you space them out and don't abuse the system. And while you may enjoy your day of recuperation, you should reserve the crazy all-night bashes for the weekends; this not only makes them feel more well-deserved but absolves you of making half-assed excuses the next day, lagging on work, and, the worst fate of all, at some point having to discuss your "problem" with the HR person, who is likely just as hungover as you are. In the meantime, try not to relive the finer points of the night before, and comfort yourself that you might lose a bit of weight!

around your head reminding you what an ass you were last night, that nobody likes you, that you're not cool and made a spectacle out of yourself, yet again, and that you're clearly not fit for polite society. If today is a workday you might have to call in "sick."

CLIMB A TREE (FREE!)

Trees. Gotta love 'em. While we may laud our leafy friends for their scenic beauty and photosynthesizing, life-bringing force, we often neglect one of the singular joys of tree-proximity: climbing! This is a low-impact way to feel outdoorsy and accomplished without the guy-in-a-Lorax-T-shirt peachiness. Scout out a tree that seems both sturdy and scalable, and begin your ascent. Bring along a digital camera to document your journey. Others may point and laugh, but they've let irony and technology turn them into empty automatons—you, on the other hand, are feeding your inner naturalist and living the life of a rakish explorer! When you get to the top, take a minute, or several, to enjoy this new perspective, writing down your thoughts in a journal that will rival Walden's for sheer nature-inspired insight. While you might be tempted to stay there forever, be sure to begin your descent before nightfall, when things get scary.

ADVENTURES IN WIGS, FACIAL HAIR, AND OTHER DISGUISES ($–$$)

Drag queens and Broadway types have known this for years—there's nothing more liberating or transformative than a big wig. You might be a natural born wallflower or just mildly socially awkward, but the magic of a really good wig is that it does all the legwork, giving you a sexy new persona without the hassle of dieting, makeovers, speech lessons, or implants. There are two schools of thought on female wigs: Novelty/Glam and Switcheroo. The former is clearly donned for dramatic effect: a bright pink shag, a saucy turquoise blue bob, a fire-engine red mane. The latter is a more realistic wig that nonetheless makes you look completely different—cascading brunette curls on a pixie-haired blonde, a short Suri Cruise crop on a long-tressed redhead. Men wary of cross-dressing on non-Halloween days should try a fake burly beard or fake mustache. These novelty items will give a normally standoffish and tentative guy a bold rush of manliness, and if the mustache or beard is too over-the-top to be considered real, a humorous, bristly conversation piece. Enjoy your new-found persona and uninhibited sexual mores—you can always blame a questionable one-night-stand on "Sasha Fierce," "Bluto," or whoever your alter ego is for the night.

THE GREEN FAERIE ($$)

 Muse of Van Gogh, Rimbaud, Oscar Wilde, and Picasso, beloved by those macabre Victorians and sadly banned in the early twentieth century by puritanical do-gooders who believe that its key chemical component, thujone, was a dangerous psychoactive drug. Were they right? Let's find out. In recent years new brands of non-thujone containing absinthe have trickled into the U.S. market, so while you might not see the celebrated "green faerie," you may stumble upon an intriguing new spirit. For a makeshift absinthe kit, first pour your absinthe into a highball glass. Then, place a slotted spoon over the glass. Put a sugar cube on the spoon. Slowly pour ice-cold water over the sugar until the drink is diluted. During this process, all nonsoluble components

(anise, fennel, and star anise) will give the drink a dreamy, cloudy quality, an opalescence traditionally called the *louche*— a fantastic French word that loosely translates to "opaque" or "shady." The addition of water is important, causing the herbs to "blossom" and bringing out many of the flavors originally over-powered by the anise. Plus, the ritual is fun and makes you look like an expert of ill repute.

MASTER THE COOL SPORTS (FREE–$$)

 Surfing is better than jet-skiing. Snowboarding trumps skiing. Skateboarding kicks the ass of Segwaying. What makes one cooler than the other has to do with degree of difficulty, demographics, and attitude. Let's face it—it's hard to look rebellious, spiritual, or tough on a jet-ski. Abandon the energy-wasting bourgeois shortcut sports and take up a recreation that has purity and youth on its side. For all three sports, you will want to seek out an instructor. As actual instructors can be expensive, you might want to ferret out the cool younger sibling of one of your friends, and hope they take pity on you or are flattered by the request. Remember that you must listen, respect, trust, and do things on your instructor's terms. If they tell you to "keep paddling," keep paddling! If they make you slide down the mountain on your butt, slide! It will be a humbling and possibly painful experience, but the great things about these activities is that the payoff is mighty. The first wave, the first jump, the first trick will lift you into a state of euphoria and childlike wonder. This feeling is addictive, and you should feed the addiction as necessary.

UNDERGROUND HAIR PARTY ($$)

The next time you're sitting in the chair of your posh salon, getting a killer haircut, look around: Kartel light fixtures, marble floors, exquisite tile work in the washing bowls. Guess what: you're paying for that! Now consider a proposition for your stylist: what if he or she were to come to your place, after hours. And what if you were to round up a half dozen friends. And what if, say, each friend were to spend half the usual price per cut. Doesn't everyone win? The stylist gets new clients, as well as cash-in-pocket, tax-free payment without the salon taking a cut. The clients get a fantastic hair cut at half the price, plus the illicit thrill of the clandestine, the sense that they're getting away with something—much the same sensation as purchasing a fake bag out of a van . . . only far more fashionable.

OR . . . BE A HAIR MODEL (FREE!)

Many salons have on-the-job training for new employees, which means they need willing heads of hair on which to prove their stylist mettle. If you have a relatively low-maintenance look and want a free haircut, styling, or color treatment, contact the swankiest salon in your area and ask if they are in need of hair models. While the idea of being someone's guinea pig might put some people off, if you are free-spirited and open-minded when it comes to your appearance, this can be a one-way ticket to hair heaven. And it's free. The question many have: do you tip your stylist–in–training? If it's a shaky-handed slacker who butchers the job, no, probably not. But if the person seems relatively professional and sends you out looking fab, then by all means tip away.

HAPPINESS HINT

The answer to "how do you tip on nothing?" is usually $10.

DANCE OUT YOUR FRUSTRATIONS IN AN ABANDONED BARN (FREE!)

Has the man got you down? Are you feeling oppressed, sexually rejected, overweight, broke, or just stuck in a bad situation? Find an abandoned barn and just dance it out! You'll need a good, inspirational/synthesized soundtrack, so drive your car into the barn and pop in your favorite '80s tape, push play, and roll down the windows. Tight jeans, K-Swiss sneakers, a gray sweatshirt, and a single Miller Lite are all you'll need in terms of accessories, as well as a wifebeater undershirt, which is a good layering tactic—things are going to heat up pretty quickly. Do cartwheels past light-infused corridors, pound your fists against wooden slats, do swan dives off staircases and, of course, execute a perfect gymnastic triple flip from any overhead beams. Feel the injustice and rage course through your veins as you execute one aggressive, and yet artful, dance move after another until you're spent—or at least until you need to turn the tape over.

CHANNEL YOUR INNER WEBSTER (FREE!)

Devising new slang was done to devastating effect in *Mean Girls* (she's so fetch!), but it can be a fun if risky proposition to invent a new slang word or phrase and see if office underlings or social outliers eagerly pick up on it. For phrases, try the use of metaphor or simile: "That's cooler than a snow day!" When it comes to one-word expressions, the thesaurus is your best friend: "That's galled-out!" (something particularly offensive), "Ambrosial shirt!" (a particularly nice outfit), or, "That show was pudding!" (an excellent show). If you say these things often enough, you might just be able to sneak them into the vernacular, which not only means you've contributed to the continued erosion of the English language, but you've also identified who, exactly, in your social circle is a hapless follower.

Pub Crawl Pyramid Scheme (free!)

 Turn your Machiavellian sales skills into free cocktails with this innovative pub crawl model. Like a pyramid scheme, you start at the top, with just you and a friend. Find a person at the bar that seems affable (or slightly suckerish) and ask them to buy a round, promising this trusting soul that he or she will get a free round of drinks at the next bar. Continue on to the next location, and have your new friend seek out another new friend to buy a round and join your merry drinking band, promising that he or she will get free drinks at all the future bars. Continue recruiting, and getting your recruits to recruit, and you will drink for free all night, as will many of your new compatriots. Everybody wins, except, that is, the person who is the last member of the Pub Crawl Pyramid Scheme. Just hope that person is too rich or drunk to care.

Turn the Walk of Shame into the Stride of Pride (free!)

  You wake up in a strange bedroom, a digital clock on a nearby cable box says 9:15, and light slants through cheap blinds, flooding the room. There is a figure sleeping next to you, and you remember, with sudden painful clarity, that you met him or her at the point in the evening where you realize: (1) you are a fantastic dancer, (2) you are extremely sexually attractive, and (3) it's definitely time for another Patrón shot. Yikes. Take heart, a one-night stand is certainly nothing to fear. Consenting adults, sowing your wild oats, living in the moment, etc. But when you leave the scene, don't skitter out like some eighteenth-century servant caught romping in the royal bedroom. Instead, throw your shoulders back and let the morning after be a time of self-worth and wild, untamed beauty. Women, you'd be surprised how the sultry bedhead and smudged mascara can boost your a.m. attractiveness, so don't run to the bathroom and rummage around for his roommate's Clinique eye makeup remover to go au natural, which is actually much worse. Men, it's quite refreshing to see a guy sporting formalwear in the morning (and it certainly beats a borrowed pair of her previous boyfriend's sweats). Whether or not you care to engage the person on your way out the door really varies by situation—while it's polite to do the whole "let's get together again/see you around" charade of chagrin, sometimes you need to just hit the bricks. Do so with pride.

BE AMISH FOR A DAY (FREE!)

 Resolve for this Sunday, and every future Sunday, to rid thyself of any technological device. No cell phone, Facebook account, Internet access, TiVo, TV, landline, BlackBerry, Skype. No checking or clicking or dropping anyone a line. No responding or ccing or leaving voicemails or expediting downloads. Just you, the great outdoors (or the great indoors), a faithful pet, a good book, or the newspaper. Those friends and colleagues *desperate* to get your attention can wait a day. All of your emails and texts will be tucked away in their respective inboxes come Monday morning. Nothing will be lost, but everything will be gained: your three-dimensional, totally tactile, real-time existence. If that

doesn't entice you, just think about how busy and exciting you'll look to everyone who couldn't get in touch with you.

KNOW THY LOCAL STRIP CLUB ($$–$$$$)

 Most of us have been to a strip club at one time or another, usually at the bawdy behest of a self-appointed bachelor or bachelorette party planner. These trips are typically taken with a sense of humor and a grain of salt. We are all too sophisticated to really think that Brandi or Shasta cares about us personally, and look how tacky the place is: and can you believe they're actually dancing to "Rock Me Like a Hurricane"—aren't there any new pole-friendly anthems? But turn down the ironic detachment and you might find some poignant moments, unexpected pleasures, and yes, unbelievably, affordable angles that augment the illicit thrill of the strip club experience. Much like a visit to your local Indian casino, the management's priority is to get you as inebriated as possible so you will forget the seediness of your surroundings and continue to frequent the in-house ATM. Free drinks? Check. Free buffet? Check. Free lap dance? Um, dream on. While the real up-close-and-personal stuff will set you back, keep in mind you can just be a benevolent voyeur at many establishments. While strip club etiquette dictates that you should tip the dancer at the end of her main stage set, you are not obliged to make any further monetary donations unless another service has been agreed upon (e.g., an invitation to the Champagne Room). Another point of etiquette: many topless establishments have a "touch and go" policy (if you touch, you go), so definitely do not take the initiative yourself. Many times there will be a point where a dancer will approach your table to "have a drink." Instead of ogling or condescending, talk to her. Dancers usually have the best stories—ask about her best celebrity sightings or bar fights. And don't be offended if she gets up abruptly and heads to another table when she discovers you're not going to drop a lot of cash for a private dance. After all, it's just business, sweetie!

A Glock .22 and You ($–$$)

Whatever your stance on gun control, it can be a very emboldening experience to handle and shoot a gun (in a controlled environment, of course). Normal, nonviolent, everyday people visit gun ranges for fun, for self-defense, for letting off steam, and for perfecting their "Dirty Harry" grimace. Perhaps you should join their ranks!

Visiting a shooting range is a relatively inexpensive way to get the genuine bang for your buck. Many shooting ranges will rent firearms, under the condition that you come with a "chaperone" (someone who is an experienced shooter or gun owner) or are under the supervision of a shooting range employee. Since you might not want to send a group email to your circle of friends inquiring as to who happens to own a handgun, consider teaming up with a shooting range pro who will walk you through the function and safety rules, as well as lingo and posture. Most indoor ranges have ear-protection devices, but outdoor ranges might not, so consider bringing earplugs—it is going to be *loud*. And make sure you're steady on your feet— you will likely be surprised, and possibly delighted, at the kick-back a smaller-caliber handgun will cause. Keep in mind that in many cases, unless you've taken a special class, you won't be able to "practice from the hip" (draw from the holster), which might dilute the cinematic quality of your experience—but not your new feelings of confidence and secret agent stealth.

Take pleasure from someone else's achievements

"Before we set our hearts too much on anything, let us examine how happy are those who already possess it."

—FRANCOIS DUC DE LA
ROCHEFOUCAULD

Not all of us were born into privilege, but all of us can learn to bask in the secondhand warmth of other people's success. Which, by the way, looks and feels like cashmere.

BE A CHARMING HOUSEGUEST ($–$$)

 So maybe you don't have a summer home on the dunes. You don't have a yacht or a sailboat with your family crest on the flag. Do not despair: as long as you can tell a joke, order a Manhattan, and act insouciant, you can befriend—and delight in the high standards of—rich people. Once you've managed to snag that first invite, the key to becoming a repeat houseguest is mastering the "uns"—acting *unaffected* by all the polished gold fixtures and *unobtrusive* while padding around their digs. Be amenable to all activities, even if they are foreign or boring-sounding to you (racquetball at noon, a brief trip to town, then bridge at 2 p.m.!). Try to be comfortable, yet never treat their vacation home like a hotel room—tidy up, but not obsessively. Offer to cook, but not insistently. If you drink the last cup of coffee, make another pot, even if their coffee machine resembles the Death Star. Always use a coaster, don't impose your iPod party playlist unless asked to do so, and always send a timely thank-you gift or card after your stay.

Here is a quick primer for thank-you card verbiage, for those who get stumped (or just lazy):

Dear _____,
name of wealthy friend

I just wanted to say thank you for the lovely weekend

at _____. From _____
posh nickname for vacation estate   complimentary detail

to _____ it was truly a memorable
adjective-filled descriptive memory

time. You were both such gracious and _____
flattering adjective

hosts. I would love to have you over for _____
woefully inadequate

_____. Until then, I hope you enjoy the
but necessary reciprocal offer

rest of your _____
ridiculously privileged life and vacation, or some less snarky

_____.
variation thereof

Warmly,

_____
You

PRIVATE JET-IQUETTE ($–$$)

So some lucky bastard friend of yours has access to, or outright owns, a private jet. (Perhaps someone you met while houseguesting in the Hamptons!) And now they're headed to Sun Valley, and have asked you (last minute, but whatever) if you'd like to join in the ski and après-ski good times. Wheels up at 2 p.m.! What to do? First, rejoice in your successful mooching. Then, make sure to follow the basic rules: Don't overdress. Save the fur coat and aviators for your ironic "pimp 'n ho" party. You are not the "jet set"—you are merely a lucky, lucky mooch. Dress conservatively and warmly. It is customary to bring a gift to thank your hosts in the sky. Go for tasteful yet savory, such as a bottle of good brandy or high-end chocolatier chocolates. Do follow all safety rules and admire the view. Do *not* make jokes about the "mile high club" or unreasonable demands of the in-flight staff such as foot massages or weird dietary requests. While it may be in your nature to do a little self-medicating, remember that you're not on a commercial cattle-call flight to Denver; you're flying with the elite, and as such you want to both savor and remember the experience, as well as avoid drooling, sleep-talking, or feeling extremely groggy upon arrival. Once you do arrive at your final destination, make sure to follow the standard houseguest rules already described, knowing that you've already earned your fancy-plane wings.

INGRATIATE YOURSELF WITH A
KICK-ASS HOST GIFT ($–$$)

When you're mooching off of someone's hospitality, using their celebratory occasion to gorge yourself on their food, liquor, cachet, and well-appointed digs, be sure to bring a thoughtful and appropriate host gift. Save the scented candles, guest soaps, or picture frames for really desperate situations, and instead consider the quiet luxury of a cold Belgian ale. Taking a bottle or two of delicious chilled Chimay to a party is a slam dunk. The author has yet to encounter a guy whose eyes do not light up when you whip out the Chimay unexpectedly, so if your host is a male or the male half of a couple, it's guaranteed to please. It's a conversation starter and vaguely celebratory—the cork pops out like it's champagne! It seems like a luxury, something you wouldn't buy yourself, because it's "$10 beer"—your hosts will be far more impressed with your gift than if you had spent the $10 on a bottle of wine (unless the host is throwing a cheap wine tasting party, see page 37). Other kick-ass yet budget-kind host gifts include a nice deck of cards or old-school board game (Monopoly, Sorry, Clue), seasonally appropriate but low-maintenance flowers (lilac in spring, sunflowers in summer, dahlias in autumn, holly berry branches in winter), and fun but not-so-perishable edibles suited to the host's taste (box of clementine oranges, pistachios, gourmet pickles, pear chutney).

DECONSTRUCTING "BLACK TIE" ($$$–$$$$)

Black-tie events are an inevitable, and often happiness-creating, fact of modern life. Someone, somewhere, is planning an event with your name on the guest list, their fountain pen poised over the draft, about to commit to a dress code: Will it be "formal"? "Festive casual?" "White tie?" "Modern tiki?" Finally, as effortlessly as adding "fresh kale" to their grocery list, their pen smoothly inscribes: "black tie." And that, my friends, means that if you wish to attend, you must adhere to this standard.

But what does black tie mean, exactly? Do you, as a gent, have to run out to Classy Roy's Tuxedo Warehouse and rent an ill-fitting penguin suit with a colored vest and cummerbund? And do you, dear gal, have to procure a floor-length gown, opera gloves, and a tiny bejeweled bag that barely fits your necessities? The answer is yes, and no. If you have a good black suit, and a decent white shirt, all you need is a black tie—it needn't be a bow tie, just a black (silk, please) tie. If you don't have a black suit, consider this a *sensible splurge*. You will wear it to all future black-tie events, including your own wedding.

For the ladies, "black tie" tends to typify something a bit more formal than your go-to BCBG cocktail frock. For this occasion, think *vintage*. If you have a keen eye and a little spare time, it's worth it to peruse your city's finer vintage and consignment shops for a dazzling floor-length stunner. Or, to look fabulous on the cheap, it never hurts to borrow a dress from a Fancy Friend (we all have one, at least). She will likely be thrilled by your neediness—but looking amazing for free is worth her subtle pity. Be sure to not spill, smoke, or shag in the dress, and return it promptly and dry-cleaned. All of this will be worth it once you arrive at the black-tie affair. The food and liquor will no doubt be top-notch. Expect ice sculptures, glistening hams, a sushi station, and a bevy of scandalous gossip that will further secure your place among the wealthy and devil-may-care. Be sure to thank your host or hostess at the end of the night, even if they don't know who you are. You'll leave knowing that you can handle any occasion, no matter how scary or stuffy—a sense of happiness that's worth the hassle of a clothing mandate.

MAKE EVERY NIGHT LADIES' NIGHT (FREE!)

 This isn't exactly a news flash, but it's pretty easy for even a marginally good-looking girl to drink for free all night long without surrendering her phone number, dignity, or good name. Consider the free drink as a guy's investment. Investing in anything, we know, has its share of risk, in this case the risk that you'll reject him immediately after sucking down the Grey Goose. But, remember, it's his choice to play the market! Furthering this analogy, girls can take a lot of "subprime drinks" from several different guys throughout the night, bundling them into a nice, highly rated package of merry inebriation. While this lowers the chance that a girl will actually meet someone of substance, it does ensure short-term gain by allowing one to hop from guy to guy, bar to bar, happily cocktailing, without ever reaching for the check. Warning: there might be a "crash" at the end of the evening.

To amass the greatest number of cocktails with the least amount of useless or potentially misleading conversation, keep things short and sweet. Don't ask him any leading questions and, while remaining polite and somewhat engaged, don't give him the impression you are overly interested in what he's saying.

Here's a quick, easy-to-follow script:

> Guy: "Hi there. What are you drinking?"
> Girl: "Um . . . rum and coke?"
> Guy: "Bartender . . . two rum and cokes, please!"
> Girl: "Thank you!" (Sips drink).
> Guy: "So, do you live around here?"
> Girl: "Um, yeah." (Sips drink).
> Guy: "Are you an actress or a model or something?"
> Girl: "Um, no." (Sips drink).
> Guy: "Well then, what do you do?"
> Girl: "Sorry, What? I can't hear you." (Sips drink).
> Guy: "I said, what do you do?"
> Girl: "Uh huh." (Sips drink).
> Guy: "No, I'm asking you a question."
> Girl: "Can you excuse me for a second? My friend over there is trying to get my attention. Thanks so much for the drink!" (Sips drink).

For the Gents If this dialogue sounds eerily, vacantly familiar, you might find happiness by reconsidering your drink-buying strategy. Instead, focus on impressing girls with your pool/shufflepuck skills, witty repartee, or just lean back and execute your best Tall, Silent Type smolder. She might even buy you a drink!

THROW YOURSELF A SHOWER (FREE!)

 So maybe you haven't gotten around to finding "the one," or perhaps you're content with a series of "the one for right now," or maybe have even discovered that "the one" is actually you.

That's all well and good, but what about the presents? See, the secret compensation for the grand disillusionment that accompanies life's milestones is that they come with set-in-stone gifting traditions. You no doubt shell out plenty of Williams-Sonoma bucks on your happy coupled friends, but what about those who elect to remain single and childless? Whether you're a woman or a man, you have the same problem. After all, if you're an unmarried guy in your late twenties or thirties, you've rented plenty of tuxes, booked plane tickets, spent countless nights in Marriotts, to say nothing of steakhouse and strip club tabs at bachelor parties. By the time you do get married, if at all, it will likely be a dignified, intimate affair for friends and family. So it's time for compensation!

All staunch singles over the age of thirty-four should consider throwing themselves a shower, inviting all of their happily settled married friends, and gently directing them to the "registry" (Barneys, Saks, Paul Stuart, etc.). Everyone can put their child-rearing, yoga-tastic, farmer's market errands on hold and come to your apartment on a Saturday afternoon, drink champagne, give you presents, and talk about how amazing you are. You've earned it!

Tips for Your Shower Pick an item you like. It could be shoes or silk ties—it could also be vodka, gourmet olive oil, or undergarments. Just don't be too self-deprecating about it, lest people think it's one big joke. Be as formal and earnest as you would be if you were the best man or maid of honor planning someone else's obligatory event. Be droll but sincere on the invitation, something along the lines of, "Over the years I have been privileged to attend many of your events and celebrations. I am so happy you have found someone to spend your life with, to share the intimacies and grand, innumerous variety of life. That said, you owe me. Pick a shoe/silk tie/thong/etc., and see you at noon on Saturday!" Then everyone gets to watch you open all your gifts, painstakingly, one at a time.

HOST A "POT" LUCK (FREE!)

 Again, while the author can't *legally* advocate this, everyone loves it when you bring drugs to a party—but nobody wants to say so. It's just not done, socially, to request BYO Bong. If you do plan to throw a party, and feel it might be enhanced by some mind-altering substances, there is no shame in saying so on your invitation. It is crucial that you use subtlety, and remain steely calm in the face of possible puritanical reactions or mass boycott from the friends-with-kids crowd. Think of a clever little "PS" on your invite, "Party Treats Welcomed!" or "Rolling Papers Provided!" Or emboss your invites (or, let's face it, upload your Evites) with clever, modern, graphic-designed drug paraphernalia symbols. People will get the idea, your party will be the groovy freak-out of the year, and you'll most likely have leftovers, to be used at your discretion. This also works with legal drugs, alcohol, and baked goods.

STEAL THAT JOKE (FREE!)

  It's competitive out there. Even casual gatherings and simple conversations have an undercurrent of tension, as all parties involved try to out-do one another in humor or shock value. Sometimes you just run out of material, and it's at these times that it is perfectly appropriate to co-opt someone's else's hilarious anecdote, joke, or wedding speech quip as your own. This form of social mooching is absolutely acceptable, as long as you follow the rules and stay on the lookout for "crossover friends," people who may have attended the same event or been party to the same conversation when your acquaintance uttered his or her bon mot.

Appropriating Their Anecdote Change key details in the anecdote so it won't be likely to be traced back to the source. Never, ever repeat the anecdote when the originator is present, and if, God forbid, someone asks you at a later date to "tell that story again about the wild boar and the tequila!" when the rightful owner of said story is within earshot, have a quick exit strategy—namely, "Sure, let me just get another drink," or, "In a sec, I just saw someone I have to say hi to before he/she leaves!" Then flee.

Taking Their Toast It doesn't really do to give credit to the originator of the toast. For some reason, "As Sophocles once said," is a lot smoother and more acceptable than, "As my friend Ben says." So just pass it off as your own, proudly and without fear.

Jacking Their Joke This is by far the most widely accepted form of social plagiarism. Jokes are meant to be repeated; they're like modern day folklore. There needn't be a reference to who told the joke first. However, never repeat a joke you heard on TV, especially on a well-rated HBO comedy special. There is nothing worse than trying to pass off Dave Chapelle's joke as your own, and people will most likely just feel bad for you for trying.

Shanghaiing Their Speech Wedding speeches are notoriously difficult to write, remember, and deliver. If you find yourself in the unfortunate position of being a primary member of the wedding party, and have no time or inspiration to spare, hearken back to previous wedding speeches (it pays to take a notebook to jot down particularly good ones) and do a little creative homage. Make sure the details you use are for tonight's bride and groom. Also make sure the ratio of guests in attendance that may have attended the previous wedding is relatively low. Do not borrow from a speech that has been given earlier that evening.

Busting Their Moves Everyone has a friend that's a terrific dancer. They were born with rhythm, while you were born with . . . the ability to sway awkwardly, clap your hands off the beat, and execute the dreaded "white man's overbite." However, all is not lost. By observing your funky friend's smooth signature moves, you can quietly pilfer their most accessible dance floor gestures to use for your own purposes. Watch their hands: do they do something hip and ironic, like, "dealing the cards," "rolling the dice," or the perennial favorite, the "faux-vogue"? See how you can co-opt these gestures when they've gone to the bar, or are focused on some one-on-one time with a special someone. You'll be surprised at the sudden burst of confidence and freedom of movement you'll experience. Just don't attempt anything overly ambitious, like the worm, head-spin, tootsie roll, or reverse cabbage-patch unless you've had a lot of practice. You may think you're the life of the party, but you'll regret it when the video appears online.

SMALL BUT SIGNIFICANT SPLURGES

10

Give in to that little extra bit of luxury in all aspects of life

"Enjoy the little things, for one day you may look back and realize they were the big things."

—ROBERT BRAULT

A well-thought-out, expertly timed splurge enhances your happiness without bumming out your bank account.

THE MINIBAR ($–$$)

 It's a truism as old as the stars in the sky: we want what we can't have. For many of us, this truism is perfectly encapsulated in the frosty Corona and bag of cashews in the minibar. Retail price? $3.57. Minibar price? $18.95. But what is life without a little hedonistic abandon, a little "this one's for me, baby"? Sure, you could wander out of your hotel, seek out a grocery store, and stock up on late night snacks and cut-rate booze, but that's so inconvenient! And the minibar is the pinnacle of convenience. So is the pay-per-view porn, but really . . . you have a laptop.

The one problematic aspect of the minibar splurge is the part where you have to account for the previous night's damage upon checkout. It varies by hotel, but some have almost psychic abilities to ascertain your 3 a.m. ravaging of sour cream & onion Pringles and Heinekens, tacking it on the bill automatically before your departure. Smaller hotels may ask you if you took anything from the minibar, and you must steel yourself for the chagrin of admitting, "two vodkas . . . one orange juice . . . um . . . oh, and a Twix. And a Peanut Butter Twix." This is a particularly embarrassing roll call at swanky spa-type hotels, or business hotels where the people behind you spent all night denying their desire for extraneous snacks. But stand tall, knowing that the Twix/Peanut Butter Twix denouement to your well-deserved double screwdriver is *your* business, and was the key to your happiness at the Boston Southside Radisson. And beware the sinister Big Brother minibars that somehow manage to charge you for things if you remove them, then put them back unopened. Plead your case with the front desk if this happens. Justice, and your need for in-room snack consideration, must be served.

OLD-TIME SHAVE ($$)

There's no doubt that a "harkening back to the old days" trend is in full swing. Call it the new Urban Classicism—it's really just a movement made up of those weary of pleated khakis and Velcro messenger bags, guys who aren't necessarily foppish or formal but who wholeheartedly reject the ethos of "business casual" and want to bring a little savoir-faire to their everyday style. This look can be achieved in numerous ways, whether by a $375 double-breasted Civil War–inspired vest from Rag and Bone (splurge) or just an old-time shave (sensible splurge). The old-time shave is the opposite of the metrosexual's man-beauty regimen, "manscaping." It rejects the idea that men should pamper and preen themselves; instead it involves seeking out practices that are often scary and downright painful. (In this sense, they are emulating women, as anyone who's had a bikini wax knows all too well.) Involving an intimidating straight razor, a gruff barber, and a hot towel, the Shave is a throwback to the time when men smoked and drank bourbon, as opposed to taking spinning

HAPPINESS HINT

Apparently, the mustache is back, usurping the beard as a trendy facial hair accessory. If you decide that growing a 'stache will bring joy to your manly heart, be sure to consider the varying styles and shapes and what they might say about you:

The Dov Charney
A '70s pornstar homage, it can be pulled off only if the wearer embraces it with intensity, not novelty-mustache irony. Velour tracksuit optional.

The Jason Giambi
A slug-like patch of hair above your mouth. OK for aging jocks or uncles. Ideal for cops.

The Classic Tom Selleck
A bushy, yet well-maintained mustache that says "manly yet mischievous."

The '90s Goatee/'Stache
There was a period of time where it was considered cool or "alternative" to grow a small patch of hair on one's chin, connecting it to a neatly groomed mustache. Let's not revisit that period.

The Handlebar (Or, the Daniel Plainview)
This turn-of-the-century prospector look is dashing and very au courant, although it does require more upkeep, including mustache wax and meticulous trimming. A strong jawline also doesn't hurt.

classes and drinking papaya-and-flaxseed smoothies. The idea is to turn men into gentlemen. A clean, professional shave gets you at least a quarter of the way there.

When seeking your venue for this crucial (and affordable) pass to Don Draper-ville, look for an old-fashioned barber pole. Upon stepping inside, if you hear lute music, you're in the wrong place. You want brick walls and chipped tile floors, and a barber you call by his first name (which hopefully will be Marty or Hal) who can talk baseball as he's lathering up your ugly mug. You'll leave feeling invigorated, refreshed, and ready to say, "Twenty-Three Skidoo!"

OPULENT OFFICE SNACKS ($–$$)

Every office has a makeshift kitchen somewhere, a place where Bigelow tea is brewed, lunch leftovers are stashed, and office affairs are consummated. Be the hit of the marketing department by using this space not merely to heat up yet another Lemon Chicken Lean Cuisine but to concoct savory and irresistible midday office snacks! Transcend the tyranny of catered cookies and use the toaster oven to whip up a fresh batch of . . .

✕ S'Management Material S'Mores!

1 box graham crackers
4 bars Hershey's chocolate

1 bag jumbo marshmallows
1 handful of go-get-'em initiative

Break up graham crackers into 2 squares. Break up chocolate into graham-cracker-square proportions. Place one jumbo marshmallow on top. Stick in toaster oven for 1 ½ minutes or until marshmallow starts to brown. Put another graham cracker square on top of each and serve hot.

(Extra points for collecting twigs from the office park to use as tiny individual spits for the marshmallow. Do not use coat hangers or a microwave oven).

✕ Consummate Professional Caramel Corn

2 bags microwave popcorn
1 stick of butter
¾ cup brown sugar
½ teaspoon salt

¼ cup Karo Syrup
1 teaspoon baking soda
1 paper grocery bag

Pop both bags of corn, then pour both in the paper sack. Then, put the butter, sugar, salt, and syrup in a glass bowl and bring to a boil in your microwave. Stir after 1 minute, and let it boil for an additional minute. Add 1 teaspoon of baking soda and stir well, until thickened. It will turn light in color and look like taffy. Pour this mixture over the popped corn in the paper bag and shake well. Put the paper bag back in the microwave and cook an additional 1 ½ minutes. Remove and shake well again. Return to the microwave and cook another 1 ½ minutes. Shake again. Open the bag and let it cool, as the smell wafts through the office and you become the Coolest Person on the Forty-Fourth Floor.

✕ Promotion-Worthy Peanut Butter Celery Sticks

2 pounds fresh celery
1 jar natural peanut butter
½ cup chocolate chips (optional)

The peanut-butter-celery snack is fast, easy, affordable, and healthy. Simply cut up fresh celery into 3–4 inch pieces, then smear some natural peanut butter inside the celery groove. Add chocolate chips for the decadent "bumps on a log" effect. It has an elementary school feel, which is apt when you consider how cliquey and juvenile most offices actually are. Plus, you'll be surprised at the genuine glee from your coworkers when you bust them out, not to mention the additional, "it's healthy" caveat—which can't be said of the leftover bear claws and scone platter.

CELEBRATE OBSCURE HOLIDAYS (FREE!)

 Everyone loves a holiday, but what about going above and beyond the nationally recognized observances and seeking out new and unusual holidays to celebrate? Sometimes you can even use them as an excuse to get off of work.

January 6: Epiphany

The holidays are over. All the pretty lights are gone, and the festive mood has dissipated. Bummer, right? Wrong! Epiphany is a Christian feast day that celebrates Jesus' birth, baptism, and the coming of the Magi. You can remove the Jesus part if you prefer and focus on the "feast." In Spain, a suckling pig and sweet wine are served. In France, a "king cake" is served, with a small trinket baked into the cake (the person who finds the trinket is "king for a day"). In Louisiana, epiphany is the beginning of the Mardi Gras season, a cause for celebration in itself.

Late February–Early March: National Pancake Day

National Pancake Day falls on Fat Tuesday, the traditional feast day preceding Ash Wednesday and the start of Lent. Partake in this celebration of happy gluttony at—where else?—your local International House of Pancakes. Many IHOPs serve **free pancakes** on National Pancake Day (with a nice caveat that you can donate the cost of your short stack to a notable charity). Buttermilk and goodwill? Yes, please.

April 16: National Stress Awareness Day

Created in 1992, this day addresses the public health crisis of extreme stressed-outedness. Celebrate by doing something relaxing, such as treating yourself to a deep-tissue massage or yoga class, polishing the day off with a two-hour nap and "nature sounds" CD-listening hour. Avoid traffic, your boss, and cable news networks.

July 2: UFO Day

According to theorists, science historians, and geeks, on July 2, 1947, a metallic object landed on a patch of ranch land in Roswell, New Mexico, ostensibly coming from outer space. Celebrate this event with a "conspiracy theory film festival," watching every film that has to do with aliens and cover-ups, from the jittery atomic paranoia of the '50s (*It Came from Outer Space, Alien Intruder, The War of the Worlds*) to the trippier, socially conscious '70s ouvre (*The Man Who Fell to Earth, Planet of the Apes, The Rocky Horror Picture Show*), the '80s horror-sci-fi genre (*Alien*, *Predator*, *The Abyss*), and on into the computer-age conspiracy theories (*The X Files*, *Contact*, *The Fifth Element*). When night falls, whip out your telescope and keep your eyes in the sky. The truth is out there.

First Sunday in August: National Forgiveness Day

Established by the World Forgiveness Alliance as a nonreligious day of worldwide reconciliation, National Forgiveness Day is the perfect time to bury the hatchet. Forgive those who trespassed against you, whether a lover who spurned your affection, a coworker who stole your idea, a parent or sibling who corrected your grammar in front of company, or the jerky bouncer who decided you were not stylish enough for their establishment: take a deep, cleansing breath and forgive all. And if forgiveness just isn't going to happen, then plotting sweet, sweet revenge is always fun, too.

October 9: Leif Erikson Day

Channel your inner Viking with this celebration of the first European to set foot on American soil. In 1002, Leif set sail from his native Greenland on the advice of an old Norse sea captain who believed there to be land far to the south. Erickson and his men landed on the coast of Newfoundland and were believed to have traveled as far south as Cape Cod. Grow a beard or braid your hair for this celebration of bravery and Viking resolve, eat a hearty dinner, and drink bold, manly ales in Leif's honor.

December 5: Prohibition Repeal Day

After thirteen interminable years of prohibition, the Twenty-First Amendment was ratified on December 5, 1933, taking any restrictions on the sale, manufacture, and transportation of alcohol out of the hands of the federal government and into the hands of your local bartender. Celebrate this triumph of boozy democracy with a Repeal Day party, charging your guests 1933 prices for booze (hint: a beer was five cents) and suggesting '30s fashion and slang ("You're aces, toots, now where's the giggle juice at this clam-bake?")

Your Pet's Birthday

Don't neglect your pup or kitty on their big day! Prepare a special meal with fresh ingredients and/or gravy, give them treats, fashion a tiny birthday hat out of construction paper and rubber bands, and take them out on the town—visit their favorite dog park, fire hydrant, or catnip store.

SEND YOURSELF FLOWERS ($$–$$$)

 This seems perhaps a little self-indulgent, but you don't need to go for the seventy-five-dollar "Expressions of Love" bouquet—a happy little bowl of Gerber daisies is all it takes to give you a little boost, and derive curiosity and jealous glances from your neighbors or coworkers. Be sure to order them on a Monday so you get in a full week of "Somebody Loves Me!" attention. When dictating the card, keep things mysterious, but don't push it too far with any "secret admirer" claptrap, which might just make you feel more depressed once everyone starts speculating as to who exactly has the hots for you. It's best to have the card read, "Thinking of you with love, XO, me." Because that's the truth, right?

ONE FOR THE LADIES ($)

Can't afford a new dress? Reach for red lipstick and nail polish, which can utterly transform and glamorize the most plain and tired ensemble. Try Dior Addict True Red or Chanel Red No. 5. These never go out of style, and give you instant signature glamour. Especially effective for the day-to-night transition, a good red lip applied furtively in the office restroom can transform you from pallid office drone to sultry nightlife fox. Be sure to blot and always line the lip first to avoid the dreaded "clown mouth."

ONE FOR THE GENTS ($$–$$$)

Few men recognize the immense appeal of a crisp white shirt, especially in an increasingly casual culture of Tommy Bahama slobbery. But if you invest in one very nice white dress shirt (Dries Van Noten, Thomas Pink, Faconnable) and take it to the cleaners regularly, you'll have an edge on Sloppy Joe, both in the workplace and in the dating world. Sharp, clean lines give you definition and an air of success and alertness, and the high quality cut and fit of the shirt will distinguish you from the masses. And never underestimate the impact of ironing. A good once-over with a piping hot iron can invigorate even the most beaten down wardrobe.

INFILTRATE A DAY SPA ($–$$)

Spas are a splurge that few can afford on a regular basis. However, if you limit your spa visit to the least expensive treatment available, you'll get to hang out in plush, zen-infused luxury for enough time to free your mind of workday stress. For example, a monthly trip to the eyebrow waxer (women and men) will run you anywhere from twelve to twenty dollars, depending on the waxer. In addition to giving you spa entry, it does wonders for your appearance. A well-defined brow not only opens your face and enhances the size and shape of your eye, but it telegraphs "well groomed, competent, and sexy." Bushy or connected eyebrows, on the other hand, say "cave man" or "Bert and Ernie." If you pick a high-end spa, you'll get to change into a plush robe, enjoy a selection of freshly brewed green and jasmine iced teas, and feel pampered and calm, all for the cost of a bucket of chicken (or two). Other minor spa splurges include nail buffing, polish changes, mini-facials, half-hour massages, and eyelash tinting, a fast and easy process that can also save you mascara dollars down the line.

SPRING FOR THE DIRECTOR'S CUT ($)

You might think you've seen everything there is to see about your favorite films. You know every plot twist of *The Silence of the Lambs*, every explosion in *Die Hard*, and every money shot in *Boogie Nights*. Think again. The wonderful world of DVD director commentary will give you an understanding on a deeper level of the already heartbreakingly nuanced *Mallrats*. Malcolm McDowell's commentary in *A Clockwork Orange* reveals caustic humor and thinly veiled tension with director Stanley Kubrik, allowing you to feel insidery and Brit-haughty by association. Robert Redford's quiet self-deprecation and admiration for the journalists he depicts in *All the President's Men* is like seeing a movie with a seasoned, ruggedly handsome veteran. When a director and actor team up, the sparks really fly: witness the triumphant pas de deux of John Carpenter and Kurt Russell as they joke and banter their way through *Escape from New York*, or the jaw-dropping stating-of-the-obvious as Paul Verhoeven and Arnold Schwarzenegger revisit the plot highlights of *Total Recall* in an unintentionally hilarious combination of Dutch and Austrian accents: Voerhoven: "This is where your character doesn't know if he can trust his wife!" Arnold: "That's right, that's right, I don't know if I can trust her!"

PUPPY AND KITTY LUXURY, TOO ($$)

 Yes, one should always look for places to trim the fat, but don't sacrifice your pet's happiness. Consider sprucing up their living quarters— discerning dogs and cats deserve a chic, modern color palette. Paint their doghouse or litter box a trendy Champagne Beige or Dutch Blue, and repurpose moth-eaten sweaters as cashmere pet blankets. Also remember that a special pet "spa day" can be executed with little expense. Draw a bath with hypoallergenic bubbles—pick a fun, pet-friendly, non-perfumey scent like peppermint or almond. After his or her bath, deposit your pet directly in front of a heating vent or hairdryer. Then, trim their nails, give them a good brushing, and serve them dinner on the "guest china." On this note, try to avoid generic or heavily discounted dog or cat food. While it may be frugal, it's the sort of gesture that makes everyone involved feel bad. Let Buster or Piccolino maintain their Fancy Feast—because they're worth it.

GIVE YOURSELF A HAND (FREE!)

Although the author refuses to refer to it by anything other than vague euphemisms, this practice is nothing to be ashamed of. Everyone gets lonely, bored, and restless—even people in happy, functioning relationships. So, when it's been awhile since you've engaged in steamy between-the-sheets action, it might be time to treat yourself to an afternoon spate of solo love. A few pointers: pull the blinds. While your sexuality is surely a beautiful thing, it's also a very . . . personal thing. But this doesn't mean you should be hiding out in the bathroom or furtively going to town under the duvet. Sure, you don't want to make a big production out of it, that's just kind of depressing, but why not put on a little mood music and spray some aromatherapy mist? Try lavender aromatherapy oil—it has a balancing effect that calms, removes indecisiveness and emotional conflict, and creates a mellow sense of relaxation. On this note, state of mind is another key to deriving happiness from this activity—instead of being filled with shame or embarrassment, think of it as practice for your crush and a good training ground for new and exciting fantasies, such as the strapping postal worker, hot yoga instructor, shy-but-curvy barista, or the married boss with the nice arms. Also, if you engage before going out on the town, you'll find you have a nice rosy glow and a more relaxed and low-key approach to the opposite sex. Hence, love begets love.

UNDERWEAR, OUTER CONFIDENCE ($$)

 You might be perfectly comfortable sporting a vintage frock, a second-hand pea coat, or a pair of shoes from eBay, but underwear is different. Splurging on really good pairs can change your whole outlook, your posture, your confidence level, and your self-esteem. Why settle for cheap polyblends and imitation silk, which will only fray and fade with a few washes, when you can invest in a few pairs of high-quality lingerie, boxers, or briefs that, with care, will last much longer, and look much better in the sack? This brings us to the ultimate test of a sensible splurge's mettle: will it improve your life beyond the immediate gratification of a New Shiny Thing? In this case, the answer is undoubtedly yes. We've all been in a situation with a new love, or new-love-of-the-moment, and, in midhookup, realized to our horror that we were wearing the "old faithful": the tighty whities which are now sort of gray, the Victoria's Secret "Angel" bra that has long since lost its wings, the pair that sags like grandpa's undies, or the ones from college with your initials Sharpie-penned on the label. Although happiness is not usually found while discount shopping, at outlet stores, or in any place where "frenzied florescence" is the typical vibe, the hidden truth is that Loehmann's and T.J. Maxx are a secret treasure trove of reasonably priced, well-made designer underwear for all shapes and sizes. Calvin Klein, Cosabella, Badgley Mischka, Elle MacPherson are all there, and all on the cheap. And what's even better is that you needn't try them on in the horrific communal dressing room. Just grab your size and go!

It's Special Occasion Wine Time! (free!)

 You know that special bottle of wine that someone gave you as a gift, or that you and your sweetie purchased during a wine country jaunt to commemorate some milestone? It might be a rich, musky Healdsburg cab, a fragile, earthy Willamette pinot, a blingin' bottle of Cristal, a heady 1970 Barolo, or a tart Côtes du Rhône, and quite likely it's sitting on the wine rack, waiting for the right moment or perfect special occasion. Well, guess what? That occasion is right now. No matter what you're doing or what time of day, if you're reading this and near the Special Bottle, order some pizza and pop that baby open! Life is too short to keep good wine on the shelf.

ABOUT THE AUTHOR

Heather Wagner is the author of *Friend or Faux: A Guide to Fussy Vegans, Crazy Cat Ladies, Creepy Clingers, Undercover Sluts, and Other Girls Who Will Quietly Destroy Your Life.* Currently a copywriter at *ELLE* magazine, she has been a contributor to Thames and Hudson's *Style City* book series, *TimeOut* travel guides, and *DK Eyewitness* travel guides. Her work has been published in *Travel & Leisure, Dwell, Antenna,* VanityFair.com, *SOMA,* and the dearly departed *Domino.* She lives in New York City.

ABOUT THE ILLUSTRATOR

Mike Perry works in Brooklyn, New York, making books, magazines, newspapers, clothing, drawings, paintings, illustrations, and teaching. His clients include *The New York Times Magazine, Dwell Magazine, The Guardian,* Microsoft Zune, Urban Outfitters, eMusic, and Zoo York. In 2008 he received *Print Magazine*'s New Visual Artist Award and the Art Director's Club Young Guns Award. Visit him at mikeperrystudio.com.